D1453113

Rabbi Yakov Saacks

THE
KABBALAH
OF
LIFE

A much deeper look into
our surroundings

ISBN: 978-1-09836-551-6

This book is dedicated to my family
who have been my best teachers.

AUTHOR'S FORWARD

This book is based on my weekly articles that I write for the community I serve. I have been the founding Rabbi for close to 30 years at the Chai Center located in Dix Hills.

I began many books on topics of Jewish interest but have never published. Recently, my daughter Chana published a book of her own. I was so taken in by her book, and so proud of her, that I was stimulated to finally complete one as well.

Kabbalah means received since the esoteric and mystical teachings were at first handed down orally from Rabbi to student. The main thrust of Kabbalah is to make sense of why we are here. Why were we created? We need to understand the power that every human has in his or her reach. The lessons in this book are meant to empower us to be Godly and holy especially in this physical world, where Godliness is not apparent to the naked eye.

I believe that every thought of mine laid out in this book tries to reason with the reader to see things from a more sensitive place. Even if one person thinks differently after reading this book, then I would have done my small part.

Admittedly, I have used the term Kabbalah loosely. So, while much of the book was written based on my Chassidic background, some of it is gleaned from other sources and is not necessarily Kabbalistic, per se. Truth be told though, even the parts that are not Kabbalistic are still mined from deep Jewish values and insights.

If I am lucky enough that my book interests you to purchase and read it, you will see that I have no tolerance for anti-Semites. I believe in fair-mindedness and I wish to be treated justly as well.

Lastly, I believe that I have a healthy dose of common sense. I call it the way I see it but am very much open to learning.

TABLE OF CONTENTS

JEWISH AND OTHER SPECIAL DAYS

THOUGHTS ON LIFE

CORONA COGITATIONS

ISRAEL

JEWS DID NOT STEAL PALESTINE

THE MYTH THAT MUST BE STOPPED

Every time I write my thoughts on anti-Semitism, there are always comments like "all the friction and revulsion is because Jews stole Palestinian land."

It is maddening, irritating and infuriating combined with craziness and bold-faced lies.

Now, let's be real. 99.9% of those who forward the lie by commenting on posts such as mine are simply reactionary, and have absolutely no thought or research behind their stance. Like parrots, they are repeating a line that they heard from a boorish friend or something they read in a newspaper op-ed, such as *The New York Times*.

Sadly, *The New York Times* are themselves repeating what they heard from some rich investor who heard it from some oil magnate in Qatar. As an infamous renowned Member of Congress said, "It's all about the Benjamins baby."

What is the truth? What is the source for anti-Semitism?

Before I tackle the Israel issue, let us take a trip down anti-Semitic lane, shall we?

BRIEF ANTI-SEMITISM LESSON

Nazi Germany preceded the "alleged" theft of land. They killed six million Jews because of hatred that had nothing to do with a land grab.

The horrific Hebron massacre took place in 1929. They killed Jewish men, women and children with zeal 19 years before Israel's Independence Day.

Pogrom is a Russian word meaning, "to wreak havoc, to demolish violently." The first such incident to be labeled a pogrom is believed to be anti-Jewish rioting in Odessa in 1821.

Hmmm, what do the knee jerkers do with these bits of inconvenient history?

THE GRAND LIE

Now let us tackle this boorish and ignorant lie that Jews stole Palestinian lands.

Inconvenient FACT #1. Jews are called Jews because we come from JUDEA. There has been a continuous Jewish presence in the land of Israel since we entered the land following the death of Moses.

Inconvenient FACT #2. Palestine was the name given by the Romans following the capture, destruction and expulsion of Judea. The Arabs chose the name Palestine to throw the Roman victory in the Jews' face.

Inconvenient FACT #3. There has never been an independent Palestinian state.

Inconvenient FACT #4. Jews did not steal land from Arabs when they returned to Israel in the late 19th and early 20th centuries. They legally purchased land from absentee landowners living in Arab capitals to build kibbutzim and communities. Local Arab tenants were often displaced following the purchase so Jews could be hired to work the land.

Inconvenient FACT #5. The Arabs of "Palestine" were offered their own state, side-by-side with Israel in 1947. They, along with the surrounding Arab countries, rejected the partition recommendation (UN Resolution 181), which resulted in civil war and an invasion of five Arab armies to destroy the entire Jewish community of Israel. These Arab armies lost and they are still mortified and embarrassed due to their stubborn pride.

Inconvenient FACT #6. Nearly 80% of what was meant to be an Arab Palestinian state was stolen by Jordan, who is the real culprit here. During the next two decades under their control, they never gave the Palestinians independence. During the Six Day War of 1967, Israel gained that territory in a defensive war when Arab armies massed troops along her borders and once again threatened destruction.

Inconvenient FACT #7. Israel offered the Palestinians 97% of the land they claimed to be fighting for in 2000, making Israel the first and only country ever to offer them a state. This offer was rejected with no counter-offer. A similar offer was made in 2008 with the same result. Arafat did not want peace, as peace is bad for business. Arafat died a BILLIONAIRE.

Inconvenient FACT #8. Someone needs to explain to certain Members of Congress that Israel voluntarily withdrew from Gaza in 2005, removing all soldiers and civilians, giving full control to the Palestinians in hopes of peace. The terrorist organization Hamas now controls Gaza and has launched over tens of thousands of missiles indiscriminately into Israel.

Inconvenient FACT #9. The Israeli settlements in Gaza is 0%. The Israeli settlements in Judea/Samaria, also known as West Bank, is 2 – 3 %. So, don't go telling me that this is the reason for the ongoing feud.

KABBALISTIC INSIGHT

The Torah says: "Distance yourself from words of falsehood." So, when I write "Inconvenient truth," I am simply pointing out the farfetched untruths that are continuously being spewed. In telling the truth we emulate our Creator regarding whom it says: "The seal of God is truth."

In the mystical book called Sefer Chassidim (13th century) it is written that one who speaks only truth can actually change destiny by decreeing something to happen—and it will.

There only a few times that we are permitted to say an untruth. One of these times we learn from Aaron the High Priest who used to make peace between husband and wife by stretching the truth. However, the lies mentioned above in the main article do nothing for peace and only serve to further war and bloodshed.

ISRAEL DEFENSE FORCE − A FORCE FOR GOOD

Something interesting I observed on the comments on my article titled, "Jews Did Not Steal Palestine," got me thinking about the other huge myth that has gotten many anti-Semites all twisted in a knot. Truth be told, I could care less about anti-Semites. I will never be able to cure their disease. I do feel though, that I need to stop their virus from spreading to non-anti-Semites who may be negatively influenced. Therefore, I have jotted down the following thoughts.

For those of you who have never been to Israel and are getting their news from *The New York Times* or from CNN, there is no doubt that you have been fed a very biased and negative view of the Israel Defense Force. I see from the comments on my own posts as to how the IDF are demonized as killing innocent women and children.

I can tell you first hand from friends and relatives who have served in the Israeli army that this is just another variation of a blood libel against the Jews.

ISRAEL'S VIEW ON WAR

Prime Minister Golda Meir was so pained about going to war that she is quoted as saying the following, "Peace will come to the Middle East when the Arabs love their children more than they hate us. We can forgive [them] for killing our children. We cannot forgive them from forcing us to kill their children."

Another one of her quotes that is so beautiful: "We hate war. We do not rejoice in victories. We rejoice when a new kind of cotton is grown, and when strawberries bloom in Israel."

Here is another. "I have given instructions that I be informed every time one of our soldiers is killed, even if it is in the middle of the night. When President Nasser leaves instructions that he is to be awakened in the middle of the night if an Egyptian soldier is killed, there will be peace."

I once heard the following from a soldier that I wrote down. He said, "Even when we are forced to take a terrorist's life, it is not a pretty sight and the fact that we are put into a situation where we must take a human life is, in and of itself, horrible and unforgiving."

BAD EGGS

I am not so naïve to think that there are not some dirty soldiers out there just like there are dirty cops. Of course, there are a few bad eggs, but when caught, they are disciplined.

Let's take the following story as an example.

A shooting incident occurred on March 24, 2016, in the Tel Rumeida neighborhood of Hebron, when Abdel Fattah al-Sharif, a Palestinian assailant who stabbed an Israeli soldier, was shot, wounded and "neutralized," and then was shot again in the head by Elor Azaria, an Israeli Defense Forces (IDF) soldier, as he lay wounded on the ground. Al-Sharif's died a few minutes later. Azaria was arrested and the Israeli Military Police opened an investigation against him for the charge of murder. It was later reduced to the charge to manslaughter.

The soldier's shooting drew widespread outrage, including from the Israeli Defense Minister at that time, Moshe Ya'alon, and Israeli Prime Minister Benjamin Netanyahu, who called it a violation of the army's ethical code.

He was not treated as a hero for killing a terrorist who had already stabbed a fellow soldier, he instead was sent to jail as he should have been. It is very doubtful that any other army in the world, would have taken to court a soldier who killed a terrorist, even though immobilized, after the latter tried to kill his comrades in arms.

Yes, Azaria's deed is a rarity. The IDF suffers from frequent waves of terror, and is a model of restrained and moral behavior. This is the truth.

GAZA STRIP & HAMAS

Israel responded to thousands of rockets that were shot at civilian cities in Israel since Israel's complete withdrawal in 2005. Hamas rockets were not aiming at IDF bases or military personnel; they were aiming at Israel's civilian population. There is not a single government in the world that would sit back and allow this to happen for the amount of time Israel did.

The IDF sent in ground troops even though the risks to our own soldiers were great. We did not and do not carpet-bomb; we send in our troops because our morality does not allow us to NOT take into account the lives of innocent people. IDF sent warning leaflets and phone calls to Gazan civilians letting them know that due to terrorist activity and missile fire from their buildings, they are being asked to evacuate before we attack. What country in the world allows their own element of surprise to disappear because of their concern for the enemy's civilian population? Our concern for human life is exactly why our enemies use their own civilian population as human shields and their houses, mosques and schools as missile launching bases – they know how much we care.

Once again, I do not care about what anti-Semites and Israel's haters say. I am writing this more for people who are intrinsically good but are just either misinformed or misguided.

Please feel free/obligated to share these thoughts so that the IDF's good name can be upheld.

KABBALISTIC INSIGHT

After the building of the Tabernacle was completed, Moses commanded that a reckoning be made of all the metals donated for the building and their uses. Moses did so in order to be above reproach and that no one challenge Moses over a red penny.

Moses was teaching a lesson in morality. Honesty is a human fundamental.

Any two moral people can satisfy a dispute and move on. The problem arises when there is immorality involved. If one of the parties is dissolute, then attaining a compromise is unattainable.

IS ANTI ZIONISM – ANTI SEMITIC?

The question of whether someone who is anti-Zionism is also anti-Semitic has been discussed and debated for years and it took Natan Sharansky to answer this hotly debated issue.

The reason as to why I bring this up now is because as a Jew and a Jewish leader, I see a disturbing trend. When George Floyd was executed the country exploded with outrage, and rightly so. The primary role of the police is to protect and arrest if necessary. There are rules of engagement, which clearly were ignored, and this man was killed by a rogue cop.

This led to cries of racism and protests to demand accountability once and for all. Too many blacks are killed by the hands of police officers and it needs to stop. (The fact that it led to riots, looting and all sorts of criminal behavior unfortunately distracted many from the message). The message clearly was and is, Black Lives Matter and they do with certainty. All the people that I know are so outraged over this murder. A life snuffed out on a whim and Mr. Floyd is not the only one.

What happened next is disturbing. In many of these protests in multiple states and countries, protestors drew a comparison between the Black Lives Matter movement engulfing the U.S. and the plight of Palestinians in Israel and the occupied territories. Essentially, two struggles that have joined together to bring awareness of the oppressed.

This led me to the question and clarification of when is anti-Zionism – anti-Semitism?

Let's be clear. Anyone at any time can criticize Israel. Just as it is okay to disapprove of any country in the world, one is allowed to disparage Israel. This small country has done some incredible things but it is not perfect. There have been plenty of mistakes and gross lapses of judgment over the years, and we hope that Israel learns from them.

What is not okay, however, is to extend this disapproval of Israel to all Jewish people. Common sense tells you that while you may dislike the dictator of Korea, it does not mean you hate every Korean. Sadly, in many of the rallies world-wide, the haters conflated their revulsion of Israel with the hatred of Jews and comparing Jews to Hitler, as in one notorious Brooklyn rally in 2020.

In addition, the claim that Israel can no longer exist is expressed by "From the River to the Sea" and is clearly anti-Semitic (UN Article 1& 161).

Human rights activist Natan Sharansky clarified for us when anti-Israel amounts to anti-Semitism by using the "3 Ds" criteria. I thank Allan Richter for educating me in this regard.

The first "D" is the test of demonization by blowing Israel's actions out of all sensible proportion, such as comparing Israelis and Nazis.

The second "D" is the test of double standards, which examines when criticism of Israel is applied selectively, while real human rights abuses by known abusers such as Cuba, Venezuela and Syria are ignored.

The third "D" is the test of delegitimization—when Israel's fundamental right to exist is denied, alone among all peoples in the world.

So, now that we know the three "Ds" let's examine what happened over the past few weeks and you be the judge.

BROOKLYN – JULY 2020

At a Brooklyn "No to Annexation" rally, speakers call to abolish police, Israel, and the U.S. Government. Crowd chants: "Death to America!", "Millions of Martyrs Are Marching to Jerusalem!" Activists shout: "When a Precinct or a Cop Car Burns, It Feels Closer to Palestine."

BRUSSELS - JUNE 2020

Around 500 people, some waving Palestinian flags, rallied around Place du Trône to denounce plans to apply Israeli sovereignty to parts of the West Bank, and called for a boycott of Israel and the implementation of international sanctions against the country. But a video shared on Twitter shows protesters shouting anti-Jewish slogans in Arabic and calling for the murder of Jews.

SAN DIEGO – JULY 2020

On its Facebook page, the Palestinian Youth Movement issued directions for a "car caravan route" in San Diego to avoid violating Coronavirus restrictions. Among the sites on the route were an office of the Anti-Defamation League (ADL), the American Jewish women's organization Hadassah, and the Hillels at the University of California San Diego and San Diego State University, none of which are Israeli organizations.

BOSTON – JULY 2020

In Boston, about three hundred people associated with BDS Boston chanted Hamas slogans in front of the offices of the local ADL branch and the Jewish Community Relations Council (JCRC).

Camera analyst Dexter Van Zile said about the Boston protest, "Kaffiyeh-wearing college students and mostly middle-class white activists with Palestinian flags were shouting for the violent elimination of the world's only Jewish state. Think about that: they're chanting eliminationist rhetoric outside the offices of mainstream American-Jewish organizations – a fact which shows that this wasn't simply about Israel, but about Jews as Jews."

Other "Day of Rage" events took place in Chicago, New York City, San Francisco, and Washington, DC.

There are two reasons why I am writing these thoughts.

1. The Jewish voice is mostly silent to this oppressive voice of hate of Jews and Jewish establishments. Silence is extremely dangerous because if there is no voice now, then there may be no voice in the future.

2. To state clearly to all pro-justice and equality movement that it makes no sense to fight prejudice with further prejudice. NONE. We are on your side and we of all people completely understand your pain. If you continue aligning with anti-Semites, you will lose your cause.

KABBALISTIC INSIGHTS

For a Jew, the Land of Israel is more than a place. It is the soul of the people. A Jew does not travel to Israel, but returns there. Israel is not just like any other land; it is called the Holy Land. In fact, it is more than the "Holy Land", it is also the "Promised Land." God promised this land to Abraham, Isaac, Jacob and to the Jewish people after the Exodus and countless other times.

For someone to claim that Israel or parts thereof does not belong to the Jews, it strikes at the core of our beliefs, practice and history, and goes against the law.

ORTHODOX JEWS WHO DESPISE ISRAEL!!

A STRANGE BREED

My latest few columns have been on Israel. Many of the comments posted mention Orthodox Jews who oppose Israel. Most of the comments are from people who are bewildered as to how religious Jews can be for the destruction of Israel. Others capitalize on the fact that there are Jews who despise Israel and use it somehow as proof that Israel is evil because, "the most religious among them know the real truth."

Truth be told there are plenty of Jews who are opposed to Israel on religious grounds. Take the Satmar sect of Chassidim as an example. They oppose Israel on religious grounds and not political ideology. The Satmar Rebbe wrote a thesis as to why Jews should still be living in exile and not have an established state, and not rush God's hand in this. Agree with them or not, they would NEVER argue for the destruction of the Jewish people and the State. The Satmar Rebbe, in fact, does visit Israel. The Satmar, to their credit, do not receive any subsidies from the State, as they do not wish to be hypocritical.

The group of Jews that are commented about are called Neturei Karta. This group unlike Satmar and others who don't like the fact that Israel is secular, are psychos, as you will soon read. They have committed acts of treason against Israel and in my opinion, the Jewish people.

Many Orthodox Jewish movements, including some who oppose Zionism, have denounced the activities of the radical branch of Neturei Karta. It is important to point out that the NK are not a Chassidic sect, even though they look and dress like Chassidim.

SPYING

In July 2013, the Shin Bet arrested a 46-year-old member of Neturei Karta for allegedly attempting to spy on Israel for Iran. As part of a plea deal, the man was sentenced to 4 ½ years in prison.

FLAG BURNING

I always get upset when I see a Muslim light a flag of Israel or one of the U.S. I get incensed when I see a fellow Jew do the same. If you take a look (not that you should) at the Neturei Karta's website, it proudly shows its members participating in public burning of the Israeli flag. Maddening.

FARRAKHAN

In January 2000, members of the NK met with Louis Farrakhan, who has been accused of inciting anti-Semitism and of describing Judaism as a "gutter religion" and calling Jews "Termites."

PALESTINIANS

Two of its members participated in a 2004 prayer vigil for Yasser Arafat outside the Percy Military Hospital in Paris, France, where he lay on his death-bed. An impressive contingent attended Arafat's funeral in Ramallah.

Almost a year after the Gaza War, a group of Neturei Karta members crossed into Gaza as part of the Gaza Freedom March to celebrate Jewish Shabbos to show support for Palestinians in the Hamas-ruled enclave.

IRAN

To me one of the worst acts of treason they have committed was when in March and December of 2006, several members of a Neturei Karta's faction visited Iran where they met with Iranian leaders, including Ahmadinejad whom they praised.

What this group did in December 2006 was terrible. Members of Neturei Karta, including their spokesperson, Yisroel Dovid Weiss, (refuse to call him Rabbi) attended the International Conference to Review the Global Vision of the Holocaust, a controversial conference being held in Tehran, Iran, that attracted a number of high-profile Holocaust deniers.

In his speech, Weiss explained that while the Nazi Holocaust was certain and irrefutable, he claimed that Zionists had "collaborated with the Nazis" and "thwarted…efforts to save…Jews," and expressed solidarity with the Iranian position of anti-Zionism. Rabbi Yonah Metzger, the chief Ashkenazi Rabbi of Israel, immediately called for those who went to Tehran to be put into 'cherem,' a form of excommunication.

CHABAD

I guess it gets very personal to me when one of the targets of the 2008 Mumbai attacks was the Nariman House, which is operated by the Chabad movement of which I am a part. Neturei Karta, instead of mourning the loss of life, issued a leaflet criticizing the Chabad movement for its relations with "the filthy, deplorable traitors – the cursed Zionists that are your friends." It also lambasted Chabad organizations for allowing all Jews to stay in its centers, without differentiating "between good and evil, right and wrong, pure and impure, a believer and a heretic." The very foundation and tenet of our entire philosophy is not to differentiate between Jews and be available for all.

The bottom line is this:

These people cannot and should not be taken as any barometer of the Jewish people. They are a marginalized group whom even anti Zionists groups have shunned. They are less than a few hundred in number, who seek to destroy instead of to build. The only reason I bring them up instead of ignoring them completely is because the anti-Semites love to quote them, when in reality, they are nothing but lunatics.

Let's try not to bring them up again.

KABBALISTIC INSIGHT

To simply err is human. To err in masses is tragic and dangerous. To err and side with those that wish you and your family and people dead is craziness and has no credibility whatsoever.

There were treasonous Jews in the times of the exodus from Egypt.

There were many holy Jews in the former Soviet Union that defied the law that prohibited Yeshivas, circumcisions and Matzah on Passover. To stand up for one's faith is considered holy act. To stand against one's faith is unholy and debauchery.

CAN THERE BE PEACE?

A NEW UNITY

Recently, the United States changed their policy with regards to Israel and to areas called the West Bank also known as Judea and Samaria.

The Trump administration declared that the United States does not consider Israeli settlements in the West Bank a violation of international law, reversing four decades of American policy.

This decision reversed a 1978 legal opinion by Jimmy Carter's State Department concluding that the settlements were inconsistent with international law. Mr. Pompeo said that Carter's ruling "hasn't advanced the cause of peace."

Truth be told, there is nothing that Jews or Israelis can do to advance peace. Pretty much nothing short of moving back to the crematoriums.

WE CANNOT MAKE PEACE

There is not one concession ever made with Palestinians that brought peace.

Israel's COMPLETE withdrawal from Gaza in 2005, where not one Jew remained (Hitler's dream – no?) was rewarded just over a year later with a Hamas victory. Israel has been barraged with thousands upon thousands of rockets, and unfortunately, until the ruling party there, Hamas, changes its policy of acting as both a government and a terror organization, which even the spineless U.N. agrees that they are terrorists, Israel and her citizens will not be secure.

THE GREAT UNTRUTH

The media such as the NY Times, Palestinians, and the United Nations may tell you that the "settlements" are a main sticking point in peace negotiations that have failed to find a solution for generations. The aforementioned will also remind us that only a two-state solution can and will work. Read on. Regrettably, this is an untruth.

THE RECENT EYE-OPENING RALLY

As the Palestinian Islamic Jihad fired hundreds of rockets at Israeli civilian communities last week, a coalition of supposed peace groups organized a Times Square rally to make their position clear.

The rally was sponsored by American Muslims for Palestine (AMP), Within Our Lifetime and Al-Awda: The Palestine Right of Return Coalition. They did not call for an end to violence. Instead, they endorsed it as a means to eliminate the state of Israel. Read on.

THE GREAT TRUTH

Read carefully what they were chanting and saying and you will have to conclude that only our death will satisfy these people.

"One, two, three, four… Occupation no more," they chanted. "Five, six, seven, eight. Smash the settler Zionist state."

"We don't want two states. We want '48."

"From the river to the sea, Palestine will be free."

Both chants call for Israel's elimination, with "'48" referring to the year Israel was created, and a Palestinian state "from the river to the sea" would cover all of what today is the world's only Jewish state.

American Muslims for Palestine (AMP) is a virulently anti-Israel group and one of the principal advocates of the Boycott, Divestment, and Sanctions (BDS) movement against the Jewish state. It routinely sponsors conferences that serve as a platform for Israel bashers, and openly approves "resistance" against the "Zionist state."

Sayel Kayed, from AMP's New Jersey chapter, made sure there was no confusion about protesters' ultimate goal: "You know, people ask, 'does Israel have a right to exist?'" "No!," he screamed. "Israel has no right to exist on Palestinian land."

He then led the crowd in a chant:

"Does Israel have a right to exist?"

"No!"

"Does Israel have a right to exist?"

"No!"

"Does Palestine have a right to resistance?"

"Yes!"

"Does Palestine have a right to resistance?"

"Yes!"

"Palestine, is all of Palestine, from the river to the sea…. Give us our land back and you will have peace. Otherwise, resistance 'til the end, 'til every inch of Palestine is free. Free, free Palestine!"

IN CONCLUSION FOR NOW

I know that there are organizations and even Jewish organizations like Code Pink & J Street are mortified that we have been given a gift by Mike Pompeo which legitimizes Jewish communities to settle and build houses in areas that were not allowed under Carter. To these misguided individuals I say the arguments for a two-state solution is a very clever smoke screen created by a Madison Avenue marketing company. We need to stop fawning for the Palestinians love, as it will not be forthcoming as in the Gaza example. The haters want you dead or at the very best in a DP camp. They do not want Jews thriving anywhere.

KABBALISTIC INSIGHT

Jewish history took place specifically in the Judea – Samaria region of Israel. To give the reader some idea as its significance, the following is a short list of Biblical greats who are buried there.

Abraham, Sarah, Isaac, Rebecca, Jacob, Leah, Joseph, Elazar, Ithamar, Joshua, Caleb, Barak, Nun, Hanna, Samuel, Eli, David, Absalom, Jesse, and Ruth just to name a few.

To try and cancel our Jewish heritage is literally denying history.

ANOTHER PEACE PROCESS

INCONVENIENT TRUTHS

Every President inevitably gets embroiled in "peace" talks that will hopefully lead to a resolution and potential harmony between Israel and its Palestinian neighbors. My prediction is just like with all the predecessors, it will fail dismally. I do feel that it is crucial that we clear up a huge misunderstanding about the Palestinian's quest for a state. We need to understand what happened that led us into the mess we are in currently.

MYTH

Imagine you had no idea about this conflict because either you had no interest in international politics. Yet, one day as you walk through Times Square you happen upon a BDS anti-Israel protest and you inquire as to what is their gripe. They then eagerly tell you the story of the unjust occupation, and how Israel needs to withdraw from the territories. You will also hear how Israel refuses to end the occupation, and how we need a two-state solution with East Jerusalem as its capital. Bad Israelis, bad Israelis, yada yada yada.

CLARITY AND FACTS

So, you dig a little more and you discover and unearth these two astonishing facts.

1. There was no Palestinian state in 1967 or any time before that. 2. Israel did not occupy East Jerusalem, The West Bank and Gaza any time between 1948 and 1967! READ THAT AGAIN. Israel did NOT occupy Jerusalem and the other territories. Wow.

You will then ask yourself and wonder, why Abbas and Arafat did not declare a Palestinian state during the 19 years between 1948 and 1967. They had over 19 years days to declare a state but failed to do so.

What you discover in a non-Palestinian text book, is that Israel declared a state in May of 1948 on the VERY same date that the British Mandate expired. So, one state gets declared within a few hours and the other state cannot get its act together over the course of 19 years! You are totally confused. You conclude that maybe the bad Israeli is really not so bad and that the BDS creep is either ignorant or is evil. Either way, not good.

You then must come to the only logical conclusion. The Israelis wanted their part of a two-state solution, but the Palestinians did not.

Abbas, Arafat and the other "leaders" refuse to speak about the times between 1948 and 1967. Abbas chooses rather to play to the gallery at the UN rather than be an honest and peaceful leader and end the self-afflicted refugee crisis that he and his predecessors created in the first place.

You also find out that Palestinian Liberation Organization was founded 1964 which was three years before the six day war!!

REASONS FOR THE CHARADE

So, why do I think that this round of peace talks will also fail?

Simply put there is no money/personal gain in peace. We constantly hear about the economic misery of the Palestinians and the high unemployment rate. What we do not hear about are the rags to riches stories and the miraculous economic achievements of some of the Palestinians.

Yasser Arafat upon his death was estimated to be worth anywhere between $1 - $3 billion (not shekels or the Palestinian currency). He was amazing at diverting funds that were supposed to go to the poor people.

President Mahmoud Abbas is not quite as savvy but still has $100 million as of 2014. He also has a private jet worth $50 million. Due to political pressure, he had to give up his $17 million palace and converted it to a museum. Shame.

Abbas is a great father though because he helped his sons own their own businesses valued in excess of $300 million. The sons' company is called Falcon and they rule the West Bank.

Falcon owns the following:

Falcon Cigar and Tobacco.

Falcon Electricity and Mechanical with offices in Jordan and the UAE.

Falcon Media Company

Falcon Investments

The industrious Abbas also owns Al-Mashrek insurance company with 11 branches as well as Al-Khayar al-Awal development company.

We would be remiss if we did not mention the famed "businessman" Hassan Nasrallah, the leader of the Lebanese terrorists Hezbollah who has amassed a personal net worth of $250 million.

So, the next time you shake your head about the economic plight of the poor Palestinians, please try and recall the illustrious Arafat, Abbas and Nasrallah families and you will fully understand why peace is not possible.

KABBALISTIC INSIGHTS

The Talmud asks the following, "Why are the letters of the word sheker (falsehood) adjacent to one another in the alphabet, while the letters of emet (truth) are distant from one another? That is because while falsehood is easily found, truth is found only with great difficulty."

The Talmud then points out that the shape of the letters that comprise the word sheker (falsehood) all come to a point to look like they are on one foot. But the letters that comprise the word emet (truth) stand on bases that are wide like bricks?

The Talmud concludes because the truth stands eternal and falsehood does not.

HOLOCAUST

TO TEACH OR NOT TO TEACH

There have been over 80 anniversaries of Kristallnacht, the night of broken glass commemorated. Most historians argue that this was the beginning of the end for Jews living in Europe as Kristallnacht was sanctioned by the highest echelons of government. The beatings, killings, destruction and burning were all encouraged by the Nazis and their cohorts.

I was positing to myself the following conundrum. A dangerous pastime.

On the one hand, it is no wonder why we are losing our youth's interest in Judaism. If our Judaism is relegated to the Holocaust, then why would a kid want to be associated with death, destruction, martyrdom and victimhood? On the other hand, the Holocaust happened and the phrase "Never Again" is more than just a slogan. It is a vow to never allow ourselves to be marginalized by any government or group of people.

So, what to do? To teach or not to teach – that is the question.

The Holocaust is indeed central to Jewish education, Jewish history and Jewish discussion – as well it should be – especially when there are those who seek to heap indignity upon the memory of the six million by trying to deny what happened and erase the lessons that must be learned and never forgotten from that very dark stain on human history.

However, let us put this into perspective. It is not the horrors, the torture, the sadism, the suffering and the genocide of the Holocaust that defines who we are! We do not share those stories to make the point that we are the world's victims. On the contrary! All the stories are intended to reinforce the fact that we are victors. The real thrust of the stories is not that we suffered, but that we survived; not that we died, but that we are alive!

This, to me, is the message of the Holocaust.

I believe that the best way of honoring the memory of the six million is by keeping alive the ideals and values that they lived for. What a tragedy it would be if we were simply reduced to being known as victims of society.

Yes, the memories are sacred. It is what we do with those memories, however, that needs to be more clearly understood. A philosopher once famously said that Judaism has 613 commandments… "The 614th commandment," he said, "is to deny Hitler any posthumous victories." Reducing Jewish identity to victimhood would be such a victory – and we must not allow that to happen!

We are not victims! We are victors!

We are the architects, builders and educators of human civilization. This country was based on Judeo values. We are the teachers and we are the inspiration for our founding fathers. No victims here!

Aside from being the Rabbi at The Chai Center, I am the director of the NY Friendship Circle. The NY Friendship Circle (www.NYfriendshipcircle.com) exists to create meaningful relationships between children and teens with special needs and typical children and teenagers. This pairing teaches all involved that we need to celebrate their individuality. It increases confidence, ignites dreams, and redefines worldviews for all parties. These children and their families could go around seeing themselves as victims, but they do not because they are not.

These children with special needs are not victims, they are children.

Furthermore, these children through our unique formula introduce teenage volunteers to something so rich and pure. Ask any typical teenager involved in The NY Friendship Circle if they think the child they hang out with is a victim. They will respond with a resounding no.

This is in line with the philosophy that victimhood has never been, and is not now, the foundation of anyone's identity.

KABBALISTIC INSIGHT

The following was written by the Lubavitcher in Rebbe, Rabbi Menachem M. Schneerson in 1979 long before anyone used the term "special needs."

"I am quite convinced that if a proper system of aptitude tests were instituted, to determine the particular skills of our special children at an early age and appropriate classes were established to enable them to develop these skills, the results would be enormously gratifying, if not astounding.

Needless to say, such an educational method would greatly enhance their self-confidence and general development, not to mention also the fact that it would enable them to make an important contribution to society.

CAN THE HOLOCAUST HAPPEN AGAIN?

I once wrote an article positing that we should not use the words Nazis, Holocaust and Gestapo flippantly. I found that many were referencing these terms when talking about certain political figures, which I felt was cheapening the death and suffering of Jews in Nazi Germany.

A few people asked me, or better yet challenged me, as to whether I was advocating that a Jewish Holocaust can never happen again and it was a one-time event. Therefore, for clarity, I offer the following thoughts.

There are those who feel we have come a long way since Nazi Germany and my response to this is, have we? Really? Just recently the U.N was asked to condemn Hamas, which is a listed and known terrorist organization, and they could not bring themselves to do this. To add insult to injury this was just days after a pregnant Jewish woman was shot and ultimately killed by a Hamas terrorist. If the U.N cannot condemn open and shut cases of murderers of Jews, then I ask you to analyze how far have we come. My response is therefore that we have not come far at all. In fact, it is my belief that the U.N. not only does not advance peace and tranquility, it promotes anti-Semitism by its very existence.

There are those who do argue that a Jewish Holocaust can never happen again due to the fact that we live in a 24-hour news cycle and the media are embedded in every dark corner of the world.

I completely disagree with this notion and this is why.

Take the War in Darfur, a major armed conflict in the Darfur region of Sudan that began in February 2003 as an example. The Sudan Liberation Movement and the Justice and Equality Movement rebel groups began fighting the government of Sudan, which they accused of oppressing Darfur's non-Arab population. The government responded to attacks by carrying out a campaign of ethnic cleansing against Darfur's non-Arabs. This resulted in the death of hundreds of thousands of civilians and the displacement of close to another half a million people. This war lasted until 2010, which is only a few years ago!!

If 300,000 people can be killed in front of the media and hundreds of reporters all because of their beliefs only a few years ago, do you really think that this cannot happen here? The truth is, in my lifetime there have been multiple genocides and atrocities that have been committed. Off the top of my head I can think of the Yazidis, the Cambodians (3 million people), the Bosnians, the Rwandan, the Bangladesh (2 million plus), the Isaaqs, the Kurds, the Myanmar and who can forget the Hutus and the Tutus.

So, no, I am not so naïve as to believe that a Holocaust can never happen again and yes, we have to do everything in our power to assure that it does not. Please realize however, that the U.N is probably the last place we should look to for help. And while the media cannot help during an active genocide, they can and should be used to prevent one from happening.

So, having read this morbid thought you may feel saddened or fearful. This is the last thing I wish to accomplish with these thoughts.

Therefore, I offer this in conclusion. To prevent large injustices from happening, one needs to prevent or at least object to smaller ones.

Case in point: There is something I lived through and I still get angry when I think about it due to the apathy that reigned. I am talking about the Crown Heights riots. I moved out of Crown Heights coincidentally two weeks after, but what I witnessed was something that was shameful.

There were three days of riots where Jews were being targeted and the police were ordered by Mayor Dinkins to "let them vent their rage" and show restraint. My wife and I were afraid to walk the streets especially after 6 P.M. This insanity went on for days and while the newspapers reported it, I did not witness EVEN ONE vanload of good and moral people coming to the defense of the Jewish people. Can you imagine if 3,000 people showed up and said this atrocity is not going to happen anymore? What a message that would have sent?

Alas, no one showed and no one cared. The lesson here is that we need to be vigilant and caring. If there are people who are being unjustly targeted, then you and I need to get up off our chairs and get there to assist.

I personally regret not running to Pittsburgh to show my support.

Whatever our individual circumstances in life may be, let us not see our struggles and challenges as obstacles to our achieving a true sense of happiness and fulfillment in life. On the contrary, let us see them as opportunities to propel us to newer and greater heights in all aspects.

DEEPER INSIGHT

In his writings and discussions on the subject, the renowned scholar and Kabbalist, the Lubavitcher Rebbe, Rabbi Menachem M. Schneerson rejected all explanations for the Holocaust. What greater conceit — the Rebbe would say — and what greater heartlessness, can there be than to give a "reason" for the death and torture of millions of innocent men, women and children?

There are things that happen in this world that are unanswerable as the human mind is finite and the Creator is infinite. Only God Himself can answer for what He allowed to happen.

MENTAL HEALTH & UPKEEP

THREE WAYS TO TACKLE MENTAL HEALTH – FOR THE CAREGIVER

As a Rabbi, I encounter my fair share of mental health concerns, from parents who are struggling with their children who have issues to troubled spouses to grown adults who are dealing with parents who have been stricken with dementia, Alzheimer's, paranoia and depression.

Recently, there has been an explosion of mental health crises due to COVID. The lockdowns, isolation, loss of income and lack of socialization has wreaked havoc worldwide. I recently read that there have been more suicides in Japan than COVID-19 deaths.

Seeing and hearing about so much distress prompted me to share the ensuing reflections. Truth be told, the following musings apply to any parent or caretaker and not just to the mentally ill. I may not be allowed to dispense or prescribe drugs and therapeutics, but life experience, combined with various courses and having an extremely brilliant spouse, has taught me some basic fundamentals that can help any caretaker.

SELF CARE

It is imperative to remember that the caretaker also needs care. It is deleterious to one's health to absorb crisis after crisis without looking after oneself. If charity begins at home, then surely personal health does as well. A caretaker is no good to anyone if they are exhausted, frazzled, mentally fried, and saturated with negativity. Take a guilt free break and do so as often as you need to. There is no Mitzvah in participating in "caretaker marathons." It is not noble nor is it productive. Take some time off and get in a nap, salt bath or listen to one of my classes online. (My classes are world renowned as a cure for insomnia.)

DON'T SHOULDER BURDEN ALONE

Another fundamental is to always make sure you have a partner to help with these most complex issues. If you are dealing with a parent, then make sure that you are not the only one handling this. Bring/shlep a sibling along with you. It makes such a difference if there are two of you making difficult decisions rather than just one. If there are no siblings available then bring along a friend or even consult/hire a mental health professional to assist you in navigating these turbulent waters.

If the issue is with a child, then both parents must be involved. One parent must not be allowed to shirk responsibility, as it is simply unfair and not as efficacious as both parents being on board. It is also imperative that parents convey the same message to their kids at all times. Parents need to be a united force. This is true in general but especially so in a mental health case. Parents must work out their disagreements behind closed doors out of earshot of any of the kids.

It is written in the holy Kabbalistic works of Tanya that when two people come together to conquer an issue or solve a problem, then the two individuals gain power from each other and they are able to overpower the issue and find a solution to the often-elusive resolution.

DEPROGRAM/DECOMPRESS

Caring for someone with mental illness is like nothing else. Things that are normal and conventional are thrown out the window and many caretakers lose their equilibrium. At some point, if not addressed, caretakers can begin to wonder if they are losing it themselves. In addition, after witnessing many morose and unbelievable incidents, the caretaker can become depressed and nonfunctional. This is why it is vital for the caretaker to have a caretaker. Someone who they see professionally to help them deprogram the events of the past few weeks or months. Speaking to someone about what you saw, experienced and felt is a proven method to assure that you, the caretaker, does not fall into a dark place.

A CONCLUDING BLESSING FOR THE CARETAKER

May the Almighty look down upon you and see your compassion, empathy, kindness and generosity of spirit, and may He reciprocate in double measure. May your pain and the pain of your beloved be mitigated. With blessings that the darkness and the dark moments be replaced by happier times filled with positivity.

KABBALISTIC INSIGHTS

Every person has the ability to bless. We are taught in the Kabbalah that the Hebrew word for blessing is Bracha which shares a common root with breicha, which means "wellspring." In essence a blessing opens a wellspring of blessing that flows down from the heavens.

Through a blessing you can turn a mundane experience into a holy one. When you visit a loved one who is ill, offer a blessing for healing. Imagine the strength and comfort such a blessing would bring.

VOTE FOR CHANGE

AN INTERNAL TRANSFORMATION

This is an election year, and all the politicians are pitching their thing, all vowing to change the country, state, city or town. I personally cannot wait until it is all over, as I can barely hear myself think with all the noise coming from every angle. I pray every day that whoever wins shall have the tenacity to get us through the next four years and beyond safely and happily.

All this talk of change got me thinking. The High Holy days are only a month away and one of the "conditions" for a happy and healthy year is for us individually and communally to change our old ways and bad habits picked up throughout the year, and instead, embark on a brighter and better journey with positive goals, aspirations and ambitions.

To change one's life for the better, whether spiritually, emotionally, socially, or even your career or marriage, is a difficult task indeed. It takes much effort, discipline and determination. The best way to go about achieving change is to follow a few simple but yet very important steps.

GO SLOW

Do not try to change everything at once. Proceed slowly and prioritize. Break the big picture goal down into systematic, manageable baby steps. Then, document and celebrate your wins daily. Analyze what things need changing and place them into two categories, easy and difficult. Pick two troubling items that need improvement, one from the easy pile and one from the difficult pile and focus in on them. If you try to change your whole life at once, you will quickly throw in the towel.

FAILURE IS NOT AN OPTION

There is no particular word in the Torah that is literally translated as failure. This is a great message. There is no such thing as failure. If you do not succeed initially, do not give up. Perseverance runs in our DNA. If we are alive today, it is because our grandparents and great- grandparents survived war, famine, deprivation and possibly torture. We all have what it takes to transform ourselves; it just may not happen in one night. Think of it this way, just because you had a bad hair day, it does not mean that you will have one the next day. Just jump right back into the ring.

MENTOR UP

Jewish tradition has been saying this for millennia. We are talking way before the 12 Step Program founded in 1938. The Mishna, written 450 BCE, states that every person needs a mentor, someone who we respect and look up to – a person who will not be intimidated to tell you as it is. A mentor is someone with whom you can share your trials and tribulations and seek advice from. Just as you would go to an attorney for legal advice and a therapist for life advice, go to your mentor for spiritual advice.

GO PUBLIC

According to the Mayo Clinic, a "strong social support network can be critical to help you through the stress of tough times, whether you've had a bad day at work or a year filled with loss or chronic illness." Sharing with a friend or two, family, and peers of upcoming changes in your life is so important because doing so offers additional benefits such as providing a sense of belonging, an increase in self-worth, you will feel supported, and a feeling of security whenever you need advice, information, or guidance.

AVOID NEGATIVITY

Rid your life of negativity.

While this is not as simple as it sounds, you need to realize that if you are surrounded by negativity, then how can you expect to have a positive and joyful life. In fact, those who are negative or surrounded by negativity are more stressed, get sick more often, and have fewer opportunities than those who are positive. It is for this reason that I cannot wait for the elections to be over. Thanks to social media, politics has become a shallow excuse for all this pessimism. We need to remove all the negativity and rise above the fray.

UNFOLLOW PEOPLE ON FACEBOOK

According to some fascinating research done by the National Institutes of Health, the researchers opine that a major factor in feeling bad and stuck ,is comparing ourselves to other people. Seeing your high school buddy's "perfect" holiday, kids or home isn't going to boost your self-esteem. It's best to remove them from your view. Don't get stuck by looking at someone's false world. Focus on yourself and what you can do to make your life better.

KABBALISTIC INSIGHTS

One of the Hebrew words used for self-improvement is Avoda which means work. It is not easy to change one's negative habits. It takes hard work. Don't give up! As the Mishna states "according to the effort is the reward."

A RECENT INCREASE IN DISORDERS

I was listening to the radio extremely early one morning this week and the newscaster was talking about how mental disorders have increased exponentially over the past few years. So much so, that the United Kingdom has established a new governmental (notice the word has mental in it) department called the Department of Suicide and Self Harm Prevention. The newscaster went on to say that globally the loss of money due to mental health in terms of loss of productivity, medical needs and pharmacy needs have reached heavy trillions (I do not remember the amount).

I asked myself why? Why over the past few years there has been such upsurge in mental health cases? I think any reasonable person should ask themselves the same question. What has changed that has caused this rise?

I, as a simple Rabbi in suburbia do not claim to have the answer but in my peripheral vision, I do see a major change in the past 20 years or so. I may be on to something.

Observation 1

Many of our children growing up today —just like many us grown-ups have endless exposure to everything and everybody with the push of a button, and this can create deep chaos and confusion. It used to be, you grew up with the friends that lived down the block, or your classmates. It was at college that you met real strangers for the first time. But today, with that little toy in your packet you have instant access to 7 billion people—and you got to choose from them. That's a heavy choice for a kid!

It used to be that there were certain things you did not share with your child as it is inappropriate and deleterious to their health if they knew certain goings on in the world. I remember one of my kids saw the video of the hanging of Saadam Hussein. It was not a healthy video and how I wished my child had not seen it. In fact, I wished that my child had not shown it to me either. It was damaging for me let alone my child.

One suggestion I have is to install an internet filter in your house and restrict access on your child's cellphone. Your child should NOT be able to go on any and every website they desire. It is unhealthy and may have long term undesirable ramifications. Furthermore, to me, a computer in a bedroom behind a closed door is a recipe for trouble if not disaster.

Observation 2

Our kids are too darn busy.

Between school, homework, Honor Society, soccer, hockey, flag football, basketball, music class, ballet, dance, hip hop, National Merit Society and who knows what else. Who has time to be a kid when you have so much else to do?

We as parents want our kids to be the best they can be, and I get that, but in the process, we have made them into machines/robots instead of kids. It is no wonder Hebrew School attendance across the Island have diminished. Who has time for yet another activity?

My suggestion is slow the heck down!! Pick one or two activities and that is it. Make American Children great again. There is way too much pressure from every avenue and it is unhealthy.

I would rather my kid be a happy kid than one that is pushed to the maximum in academics and/or sports to the point that he/she becomes unhappy.

KABBALISTIC INSIGHT

A Talmudist by the name of Rabbi Shimshon of Chinon who said that after he learned all the secrets of the kabbalah he would pray like a one-day-old baby because a child is pure and wholesome.

The Third Lubavitch Rebbe once observed that a when children get into arguments with class mates, they quickly patch things up, but adults can let an argument linger for years. He explained that an adult wants to be right and a child just wants to be happy.

EMOTIONAL FEVER

A HUMAN CONDITION

I recently completed an extensive course on human emotions and I came away with an entirely different perspective that I never had before. I was amazed that while it made such common sense, I had never thought about it in this way before. For me, it is a life changer and I hope that my readers are half as inspired as I am.

The gist of the course is that everyone understands that there are a myriad of serious diseases out there and when someone has been stricken, the family members and other caring folks gather around and do whatever it takes to help the individual get treatment and convalesce. If by chance when helping your child who, say for example has 105 fever and is in the middle of a seizure, completely by accident kicks you in the head as a result of the seizure, you will understandably never get angry and lay the blame on the kicker as he or she is extremely sick. You take the kick and you move on. You will not ruminate on how bad the person is or how he or she owes you an apology. To do so would be ridiculous. In fact, you may even laugh about the shiner you received.

In the course that I took the overwhelming message is that just as we would never condemn a sick person for their hurtful actions, so too, we must never judge a person with emotional problems.

Too often when we hear of a child acting out, whether it is in school or at home, we are quick to squash their behavior with a reprimand or a punishment. This is all well and good with a wholesome child, but how about a broken one, a child who has suffered one trauma or another? The approach that we take must be the same as with a physically sick person. Just like the above-mentioned person who has 105-degree fever, this person has 105 degrees in emotional fever.

It could very well be that we do not have a lazy child, but instead, an unhappy one. A lazy one has to be admonished and made to do chores or complete the homework task assigned. In contrast, an unhappy child needs love and not reprimanding. They need a therapy session and not a lecture. Parents and teachers need to really ascertain what is really going on. Does this child have a high emotional fever or not? This is why parents, teachers, doctors and principals need to form a seamless bond to really understand this developing human organism that we are in charge of.

Truth be told it does not really matter if your child is an adult or not. Your spawn may say something hurtful to you. Before you respond with the respect card, also known as lecture #123 from your canned talks, you need to stop, think and ask yourself the following. Does my _____ (fill in the blank) have emotional fever or are they just plain disrespectful? If they are the former then you need to absorb the kick in the head with dignity, which means restraining from the lecture and seeing how you can help reduce the fever. An aspirin is great for a physical headache but an embrace is the remedy for an emotional one.

The Kabbalah teaches us that the reason why our right hand for most people is the dominant one is that right symbolizes love and kindness and left symbolizes discipline and judgement. From here, we learn that we need to show predominantly love and kindness to all. Only if we see that this person is a "dafkanik," which is Yiddish for a bad egg who does things on purpose to annoy, then we need to bring out the left cannons, which include the lectures, detention, lawsuits etc.

After reading this, I would be curious to know what you think and what your emotional fever is.

KABBALISTIC INSIGHTS

The founder of the Chassidic movement, Rabbi Israel Baal Shem Tov, advised a parent who sought his counsel about a wayward child who does not respect the various religious laws and customs of his household and upbringing. "Should we have our child leave the house" they enquired. The Baal Shem Tov responded with something that is "No, don't throw him out, rather love him more."

A child's self-worth is worth you biting your tongue to not rebuke this fragile human.

YOM KIPPUR AND ANOREXIA

TO FAST OR NOT TO FAST

I was recently asked my opinion on is whether fasting on Yom Kippur is important these days or not. If you would have asked this question of me three years ago I would have responded completely different to the answer I now give.

In the past I would have responded with a gentle warm smile that "I don't have opinions on the Torah, I just follow the mandates of the Torah." You see, in the Torah it states that you have to fast so we fast. The Code of Jewish Law advocates that this is incumbent upon every person over the age of majority, meaning Bar/Bat Mitzvah. I probably would have added that "Please do not shoot the messenger, as I work in sales and marketing and not in management."

Back to the present. My answer now would be "it depends."

As your typical Rabbi I get asked all types of questions on Jewish Law and I answer them (when I can) according to the rule as stated in our Book of Codes. Nothing has changed in that regard. However, as a relative of someone recovering from restrictive anorexia nervosa I have become educated in something I knew nothing about and I credit my relative for giving me new insight.

Jewish law is very clear when it comes to health and safety that it comes first before anything and everything else. In other words, disregard the law if you need to, in order to save a potential life.

Let's take fasting on Yom Kippur as a "random" example. As stated above, the law is that if you are a Jewish person over the age of Bar/Bat Mitzvah you must fast. However, if by fasting, you will (even) possibly endanger your life, then fasting is not allowed. Furthermore, if you do fast when told that you must not because of a possible danger, you have now transgressed a Jewish law. Which as a Rabbi, I can honestly tell you that you do not want to break laws especially on Yom Kippur!!

I had no clue until what an eating disorder was until recently. Initially, I scratched my head with wonder as how is it possible that a Jewish child who has Jewish DNA embedded in them, could dislike food so much? In the words of Tevye from Fiddler on the Roof "Absurd. Unheard of." And then I learned and experienced the full wrath of this ...... monster that overtook someone's life like a dybbuk, demon, devil, what have you.

So, if you ask me today whether fasting on Yom Kippur is important in contemporary times or not, I answer it depends. It is ok to fast if you are healthy and show no signs of danger such as low blood sugar, DKA (ketones) dehydration, anorexia, etc. It is not ok if this will run the risk of a relapse of an eating disorder or some other disorder that will prove to be deleterious to your health.

It is not okay if you have restricted the day before Yom Kippur. It is not okay if you are using this holy day as an excuse to yourself or to others that it is ok to fast. If anything above sounds familiar, then I would say EAT WHAT YOU NEED TO EAT. I am telling you to eat not only as a human being. I am telling you to eat as a Rabbi who practices Jewish Law!!

The same would hold true with all the charity fasts that the high school and college students raise money or awareness for. Think of it this way THIS PARTICULAR CAUSE MAY NOT BE YOUR MITZVAH. Choose another cause that you can put your heart and soul into. You do not have to be all things to all people. The charity organizer may or may not understand your hesitancy in fasting, but hey, it is not your problem. It is clearly not the right fit for you.

This philosophy would apply to non -Jewish religious fasts as well. Although I am not a scholar of comparative religions, I would find it hard to believe that you would be obligated to fast if you have an eating disorder.

It is because of this very ignorance (not due to anyone's fault) that I write this short article. Please dear leader, get yourself educated on matters of eating disorders. You will be glad that you did, as to save a life is to save a whole world.

KABBALISTIC INSIGHTS

In the mystical of book of Tanya, the author rejects self-imposed fasting as a source of penance. If anything, fasting is to repair any ill feelings by God for your trespass but definitely not penance.

Regardless, the author advises that in lieu of fasting, one should give charity as in addition to repairing one's relationship with God, with an added benefit that it also helps another human being.

UNCERTAIN FUTURE

THE PROBLEM OF DOUBT

We are now over 10 months since the onset of the Covid-19 pandemic and the future is still so unclear and uncertain. Yes lockdown. No lockdown. Close schools. Open schools. While it is true that we seem to be getting closer and closer to having vaccines mass produced, there is still so much controversy and murkiness. I personally cannot wait until all this uncertainty is over and the vaccines have been fully approved and safe so we can all move on. I think the reason there are such agitated feelings currently felt by the masses is because of a concept called doubt.

DOUBT

I believe and so does Judaism that one of the worst mental issues to have is doubt. If somehow the CDC could have told us with certainty that we will have a vaccine in one year and all this will be behind us in 18 months, there would have been much less angst over an uncertain future, and we could have faced this pandemic much better knowing that the end is in sight. Of course, the CDC had no way of knowing — what we were dealing with. So, we were therefore plagued by this horrible doubt.

I once read General Norman Schwarzkopf's autobiography, It Doesn't Take a Hero, where he shares his rules for leadership. One of the last rules he writes is, "Making a decision is the only way to move forward." What struck me as I read further in his book is that even incorrect decisions are better than indecision, because a person who has made many wrong decisions has at least made a decision that this or that does not work for him or her and is now closer to the right decision. As opposed to the person who is tortured by indecision as all this uncertainty saps the energy. What we are faced with during this pandemic is doubt, which is giving us heartburn because it is so debilitating. This reminds me of a quote from the Talmud, "There is no true joy, like the removal of doubts."

QUESTION

We need to be clear though that doubt and questions are not synonymous. If we do not know or understand something, we need to attempt to gain clarity before we allow doubt to seep in and wreak havoc. King Solomon tells us that only a fool believes everything, while the wise man submits everything to intelligent inquiry before committing himself. Questioning is a path towards growth in wisdom and life. In a book of Chassidic thought by Rabbi Dovber of Lubavitch, he writes, "A person is obligated to do their best in understanding the Divine, and only after many hours of contemplation are we allowed to leave the rest to belief and faith." The reason he opines is because doubt is such a "faith wrecker" as it gnaws and gnaws at you until you become so distressed that you give up on whatever it is you are pursuing.

DOUBT II

Doubt, on the other hand, is destructive. Its victim is life itself—any effort to nurture others or self and/or to become something greater than you are today is hampered by doubt. The voice of maybe. Maybe yes or maybe no is terrifying. Doubt has no interest in the answer but rather will always revert back to the question and will never let up. Doubt is a charlatan who claims to ask legitimate questions but at the same time is disdainful of the answer. It literally steals life from you.

The only response is to quash it down whenever it raises its head. There are those who can crush doubt without any assistance from others. They are strong enough to respond to nagging doubt. For most of us however, we need a friend, peer, colleague or even a therapist. As the Mishna teaches, "Make for yourself a Rav (a teacher); acquire for yourself a friend." Most take this to mean you should pick a Rabbi and follow their judgement (Rav means Rabbi among other things).

No one has to go through life with constant feelings of doubt, misgiving, uncertainty or reservations. You have the power to change your life whether by standing strong by your convictions or seeking help from others to assist.

As far as COVID-19 is concerned, there will be a vaccine very soon and we will be able to go back to a quality and happy life without the Corona albatross hanging over our heads. Amen.

KABBALISTIC INSIGHTS

Our worst adversary comes from within. The one singular thought that can ruin everything hinder our growth is doubt. Doubt leads to insecurity and indecisiveness.

ABUSIVE PARENTS

This past Sunday was dedicated to fathers and grandfathers — a day of special recognition, gifts, hot dogs, hamburgers, veggie burgers and non-dairy ice cream with gluten free cones. According to Wikipedia, the custom of celebrating Father's Day in the United States was initiated by Sonora Smart Dodd, who in 1909, along with her five brothers, was raised by her father alone. Inspired after attending church on Mother's Day, Dodd tried to convince the Spokane Ministerial Association to celebrate Father's Day worldwide and succeeded.

In honor of Mother's Day last month and the recent Father's Day celebration, I dedicate the following thoughts to all mothers and fathers out there.

HONOR NOT LOVE

Interesting to note that number 5 of the 10 Commandments states the following, "Honor your Mother and Father." This commandment is so important that it is only one of two commandments in the entire Torah that offers a reward: "That your days may be long in the land that the Hashem your God is giving you."

Some commentaries state that in addition to a reward it is actually teaching us a lesson. You see if humanity advocates that children must show honor to their parents, then humanity will endure and have a long life. If civilization, however, does not push honor, then society will be in trouble. I know many parents who are lax in seeking respect or honor from their children and just want to be loved. However, the Torah clearly states to honor and not love, cherish, value or appreciate. Reminds me of Tina Turner's song "What's Love Got to do With it."

WHY NOT LOVE?

As a Rabbi, I periodically get the following question in some form or another. How can I love my father when he is an alcoholic and abusive to my mother? How can I love my mother when she is so manipulative and hates my wife and causes horrific arguments? Sometimes a child can simply not love their parent. It is as simple (or complicated) as that. To be clear, the Torah does not pardon a parent from abusive behavior. Judaism and most societies forbid any type of child abuse. Sadly not all societies. FGM is an example of child abuse that is sanctioned even today in some parts of the world.

Children are considered a gift from God, and were given to parents to love, cherish, educate and pass on good morals and values to the world to make it a holier place than it was when we arrived. An abusive parent essentially takes these gifts and damages and breaks them. Love needs to be earned from your children by loving your children.

THE ANSWER TO ABUSIVE PARENTS

I firmly believe that the best answer if one has an abusive, alcoholic or manipulative parent is to keep a safe distance and avoid contact whenever possible. If the abusive parent is not around and a part of your life, then, the interactions and therefore the pain, will be greatly reduced.

If and when the confrontation is inevitable, it may be helpful to emotionally distinguish between your parent as someone who gave you life, and as an abuser or manipulator or alcoholic. Honoring parents does not require honoring the sickness in them.

NOT PEERS

Another reason why honoring parents is vastly important is because children need it. While some parents may or may not want to be honored, they should want to be. You see children need to honor parents because a father and a mother who are not honored are essentially adult peers of their children and not parents. Specifically, when a child displays honor and reverence to their parents, it helps the child learn the concept of respect. This will teach our children to show deference to parents, teachers, and even God.

GOD AND PARENTS ARE PARTNERS

It is exactly this very last concept that the Talmud points out. The child-parent relationship is analogous to, and intricately bound up in, the man—God relationship. This is so because in bringing a child into this world the parents are in a partnership with God. In other words, bringing up a child without inculcating him/her with honor and respect for parents and other authority figures such as principals, teachers, bosses, supervisors and police officers, and will ultimately wreak havoc because the child will end up not respecting anyone including God.

WHAT IS HONOR

In the Code of Jewish Law, we are taught that a child must not sit in the designated dining room seat of their parents, nor their living room, kitchen or den seat. A child must not contradict and tell a parent that they are wrong but rather have a conversation without the huff. A child must not curse at a parent or God forbid, hit a parent. A child must help out in the house and should be encouraged to be a very active participant along with the rest of the family. Otherwise, you will be bringing up a spoiled child.

These are just some examples. The bottom line is that we should demand their respect and earn their love.

KABBALSITIC INSIGHTS

The mystic sage, Rabbi Israel Baal Shem Tov taught that nothing that happens in this world is random or happenstance, but rather all part of a master plan.

Souls are matched together in family units. Our parents are our parents by Divine decree. Our children were allotted to us by Divine edict. Why? Above my paygrade.

We have to do our best no matter what.

KNOWING YOURSELF IS KNOWING GOD

A KABBALAH LESSON ON SELF REFLECTION

A person who I respect who is very involved in community life told me that I am a great fundraiser. I looked at him and I said, "Who me?" He affirmed that he thinks I am a great fundraiser. I was blown away. I have been accused of many things but never have I been told this before, and quite frankly, I am still surprised at his compliment.

Which got me to thinking…

How much do I know about myself? I clearly do not see myself as this activist sees me. What else am I missing? How many other things does someone else see, think or believe about me, while I am just oblivious?

SUBJECTIVE vs. OBJECTIVE

Of course, everyone knows that there are two ways we think and see things — subjectively or objectively. Anything objective sticks to the facts, but anything subjective has feelings. Objective and subjective are opposites. Take for example journalists; they must be objective when writing or reporting news and should not offer their own opinions. They are there to just report. This does not mean a journalist is never allowed to have a view and a judgement. They can but it must not come through to his/her audience. Why? Because if the journalist thinks subjectively with feelings while reporting, then there is a good chance that the news will be slanted and biased to his opinion.

This is exactly how we operate. We, even at birth, see ourselves subjectively and not objectively. When it comes to ourselves we act on feelings. This is natural. This is how we were created. Therefore, because we think subjectively, we can skew who we really are.

KABBALAH'S TAKE

Along comes the mystical book of Tanya which says while we are made in such a way where we think individually or subjectively, we need to make time for ourselves as part of self-care, both physically and spiritually, for the body and soul, to think objectively about ourselves. While everyone knows that Yom Kippur is the day of self-knowing and reflection, the Kabbalah suggests that it be done on a smaller scale more often. There are great days and times when one should take stock of oneself in a serious effort to unravel who you are.

BIRTHDAY

A birthday I am told is the day when God decided that the world could not function without you being present. It is a day where you start your journey and assignment. No one is born redundant. Everyone is here on terra firma for a reason. Aside from your general mission, there are things that you need to do as your specific undertaking. Only you can do it and no one else.

So, every year on one's birthday, one needs to reflect. As Ed Koch used to say, "How am I doing?" Am I living up to the expectations and mission or do I need a push?

ONCE A MONTH

The Kabbalah also states that once a month on the day before the new lunar month, one needs to ponder one's life. How was I last month and how can I improve this coming one? The reason why this reflection is connected to the moon is because the moon unlike the sun is not stagnant. The moon waxes and wanes. The moon teaches us that we need to be flexible and malleable and not rigid. The moon also teaches us that we can sometimes feel whole, and sometimes not, but do not fret because you will feel whole again.

NIGHTLY

On a microcosm level, before we retire for the night, we need to go through the lows and highs of the day and ask ourselves, could I have acted differently and then tell yourself, tomorrow I pledge to be stronger.

CONCLUSION

I have been pondering the fundraising compliment all week, and I have concluded that although this person may see me as a great fundraiser, I know that I am not. Nevertheless, I can always strive for the better. Reach for the moon as they say.

KABBALISTIC INSIGHTS

The Talmud teaches that all nations count the months and years by the sun, while Israel counts by the moon. Why? The sun is all powerful and huge, while the moon does not have any of its own light?

The moon waxes and wanes and is not constant. When the moon seems to be all but gone, it experiences a rebirth if you will. This why we are count by the moon. The moon teaches us to be resilient. Just when we think we've hit rock bottom and things cannot get any worse, we bounce back up and begin again.

KABBALAH OF THE BLUES

HOW TO BEAT THE DOLDRUMS

We have all been there. We have all had the days, weeks and months where no matter how hard we try, we are unable to get out of our own head. Our thoughts race and our misery lingers. We walk around like Eeyore of Winnie the Pooh fame.

What can we do about it? How do we shake the blues and get into a happier rhythm of life? Surprisingly, or for some not surprisingly, the Kabbalah and Chassidic wisdom address this common everyday problem that plagues humanity. Do anteaters even get depressed?

This article does not address a clinically depressed individual who has a brain misfire and/or lack of serotonin. I am sure it can help but some cognitive behavior therapy, together with medication, is most effective. This advice is geared for one's day-to-day doldrums and for blue spells that affect us greatly.

In the mystical book of Tanya, the author discusses melancholy and heaviness of the heart and mind and he offers up some solutions. I have taken the liberty of breaking it down in what I call the three "tudes."

ATTITUDE

Rabbi Schneur Zalman, the author of the Tanya, posits that if we change the way we think, we will change the way we feel. This holy book was disseminated widely in the early 1800's and was revolutionary in its approach, as many believed that our characters are determined by genetic factors. Others believed it could be determined by early childhood experiences and/or conditioning.

The author, however, asks us to simply (or not so simply) reframe our thoughts by changing our attitude. He postulates that we were not brought into this world to suffer. We were born to accomplish. We are here to help others. We were created because we matter. We are alive in order to make a difference and that we need to focus on others and not only ourselves. This is something that Viktor Frankl dedicated his life to, and wrote a bestselling book about it called Man's Search for Meaning.

MAGNITUDE

Every one of us has something to offer this world. Not one of us is redundant. Just as every fingerprint is different from the next person's, so is our mission. What we were brought down to accomplish is vastly different from the next person.

When we realize the magnitude that we need to do what we were brought here to do, and no one in the world can other than you, then who has time to dwell on negative thoughts or what I call stinking thinking? You and only you can complete a certain deed, act or endeavor. You need to figure out what and when and then go do it!

FORTITUDE

If you have been faced with an obstacle to overcome that is giving you the doldrums, rest assured you were given the resources to overcome. You may need to think about it or even seek advice, but the ability to overcome is within your reach.

I am not referring to a huge obstacle like a death. In fact, Jewish law demands that you set aside time to mourn and grieve. I am once again referring to your basic lethargy and stupor.

I once saw a meme that says that the letters that form the word depression, can be altered to read "I pressed on".

Good luck!

KABBALISTIC INSIGHTS

In the esoteric book Tanya, the author holds melancholy and gloominess in extreme disfavor.

Simply put, depression needs to be fought as after all, what does depression accomplish? One can plainly observe that not only does a miserable disposition fail to correct any situation, but in fact it does quite the opposite.

LESSONS OF A SIBLING'S PASSING

SCHOOL OF HARD KNOCKS

Last week I received news that my youngest sister suddenly passed away without any prior history of health issues or any other warning signs. She was literally alive one moment and dead the next. There were no goodbyes or I love yous, or instructions, directions, or requests. Nothing.

POWER OF SHIVA

The funeral came and went. Then comes the shiva period, which is designed to make one grieve and reflect over the loss. Those who do not sit shiva, which admittedly is grueling, actually elongate the pain and emotional trauma. While I was sitting shiva and reflecting on my sister and her passing's effect on her extended family, I found myself drifting in a direction other than my sister's legacy. I instead ended up pondering some of life's lessons that I was taught upon her passing, that are also painful. I write the following not only to flesh out my feelings, but also to hopefully make it a teaching moment.

FIRST THOUGHT
POWER OF COVID

This pandemic has taken a huge physical, emotional, financial and mental toll on our lives. In these few months, many of us have given up much of what we were used to. No more Broadway shows, no movies, no Bar/Bat Mitzvah or wedding extravaganzas, limited vacations, small family gatherings and no hair appointments, etc. Essentially Covid has this huge power over us to completely change our normal trajectory. I know that I have radically altered the way I live as we all have.

Covid had such power over me that when my child got married in mid-May, which was the height of the pandemic, my siblings were not invited to the wedding, as we could only have a max of 10 people in a gathering. My baby sister did not come to the wedding, and neither did my own mother because of Covid concerns. This was the right thing to do but it was torturous. Following the wedding there is usually seven days of celebration where the extended families get to meet each other. There was none of that.

In addition, there has been no familial fraternization for close to a year, which is terrible because out of sight is out of mind. Like most, I deal better face to face. The bottom line, while not being estranged from my family, I was basically estranged from my family. What a horrific time.

REUNION

Well, the familial estrangement ended with a funeral. Somehow, some-way, by some means we all managed to have a family reunion. How can we see each other face to face? What about Covid? The answer to this of course is Covid, shmovid. When a loved one dies, you drop everything and run without hesitation. You get on a plane. You hug the kids. You hand the shovel from one person to the other. Covid lost all of its power, control and influence. After so long, we were all finally together, but it strikes me as too little too late.

The above thought is and was very painful to me. I love my sister but I was not attentive to her. I am proud of her children, but how were they to know. I kept it to myself. I can blame it on Covid, I really can. However, I really cannot. I allowed this insidious virus to alter my common sense and behavior.

I implore you to reach out and call, write, email, fax, Skype, Zoom and visit. A visit can be done safely and it should be done. I learned in the school of hard knocks that life is too short.

SECOND THOUGHT
MONOTONY RULES

The second thing I realized is that I don't know my sister's favorite color, her kids' exact birthdays, likes or dislikes. I knew her as a brother should know a sister as I grew up with her. I did not know her well enough as a mother or grandmother, wife and mother-in-law. In other words, life makes us run on autopilot. We need to first get through the day, then the week, and then the month. Mortgage paid - check. Car payment - check. Called the dry cleaners for a pickup – check. Nothing changes in our lives. If we are not careful, we exist simply to pay Chase and National Grid.

I am finally awake from my slumber, but it took a hard smack to recognize reality. We need to be intimately involved with our loved ones. We must be proactive and attentive. We need to take interest in the smallest details of a family member's life and not just a peripheral glance. We should be enmeshed knowing what is going on. Having said this, we are not allowed to pry, God forbid. We do need to be open, reachable and emotionally available all the time. They need to know your love for them. Don't keep it a secret.

Everything is still very surreal and strange. I just got up from shiva. The very first thing I did is pen this to myself because I did not want to lose one iota of emotional intelligence. Time has a habit of doing just that.

Now that I have shared this intimate moment with you, I ask you to take this to heart and share with others.

May my sister's passing be an impetus to closeness between family.

KABBALISTIC INSIGHTS

According to the Kabbala, death is strictly defined to the body. While a body is mortal, a Soul is eternal. We mourn because the physical touch has been lost. We can no longer visit, talk on the phone or zoom. It is a painful reality. At the very end of a traditional Jewish burial service, there are words of comfort offered to the mourners. The very idea of comfort seems absurd when there is such new raw pain. The comfort we are taught comes from the knowledge that death is only skin deep. Literally.

PARENTING

COMMON MISTAKES PARENTS MAKE

LIFELONG LESSONS

As a parent myself for close to 30 years I can honestly say that I messed up. When I got married, I was acutely aware of every mistake and error my parents made with me, and I vowed not to repeat the same slip-ups with my kids. Like so many of us, I morphed into a perfect blend of both my parents — the good and the bad.

I wish to address the most common mistakes parents make while raising their children. Some of them I am guilty of and some of them I had the smarts not to do or dwell on.

The following list is not in any specific order; just my free-flowing thoughts.

MISTAKE #1. CRITICISM

This is huge. When we criticize a child, even when we are doing it for the betterment of him/her and/or we wish to guide/educate them to become a mensch, it is an error. Criticism is poison to any child's self- esteem. There are ways to get your message across without destroying your child's fragile infrastructure. Common example: Your child comes home with a report card with four A's, three B's, and two C's. A critical parent will praise the A and B, but will also latch on to the C, and perhaps tell the child that less TV or less Xbox is in their future as this is the reason for the poor grade. Sound familiar? A savvier parent would tell the child in a positive voice, "I am so proud of this report card. You tried so hard. Don't worry about social studies as we will get you some help." See the difference.

I mean let's face it. When you visit your favorite proctologist, do you ask him/her for their grades or do you submit to their findings and get out of there as soon as you can. You never ask about their report card in high school and you probably go because you heard that they are good at what they do. Who really cares that this 9-year-old got a C in social studies? I never did.

MISTAKE #2. TOO BUSY

Another biggie. Our kids are too darn busy. We as parents drive them crazy. Aside from schoolwork, parents feel that all their kids are super athletes and need to be involved in every sport known to mankind. Parents take off work to see and yell at their child run, sprint, kick, throw, jump, punt, hit, pitch and slide. Then on top of that, these kids need to go to chorus, cultural club, various meetings and volunteer for honor societies. Anything leftover is for homework and sleep.

To all Jewish parents out there, let me be the first to tell you the following. There is a 99.999999% chance that your child will not get a college basketball scholarship. If you listen to me then you have just freed 10 hours a week. Seriously, though, we must let these kids be kids. Let them play with their friends on the block. Not everything has to be organized sports or clubs. Give them a break. The stress that these youngsters are under to perform all the time, is the reason we are seeing so much Prozac in the marketplace.

MISTAKE #3 CODDLING

A healthy upbringing is to allow the kids to fight their own battles. I was brought up that a teacher is always right no matter what. If a teacher called to complain about how rambunctious I was then my parents used to let me have it. I found out when I became an adult that sometimes, behind my back, without me knowing, my parents would speak to the teacher and pressure him or her to back off a little.

I taught elementary school at the beginning of my rabbinical career and soon realized that it was not my forte. I witnessed the dean of the school being tortured when parents threatened to sue over minutia, and it made me ill. Parents are supposed to support the school, and when a parent threatens to sue (over nonsense) it undermines the whole underpinnings of the institution in the child's eyes. It will also create a deleterious attitude in the child which will result in havoc.

By all means, stand up for your child, but do this privately.

KABBALISTIC INSIGHTS

The Torah tells us that Miriam judged her brother Moshe who, in her opinion, was acting improperly towards his wife Tzippora. She spoke about this to her brother Aaron, and God punished her with leprosy.

Even if she had been right about her brother's behavior, she should have never gone to Aaron. Instead of complaining behind Moshe's back, she should have confronted him directly.

COMMON MISTAKES PART II

LIFELONG LESSONS

Parenting of course begins at conception and ends when we pass on to the next world.

Active parenting is most critical from birth until the kid is about 17 because when a child gets to about 17, they have already been molded, scarred and prepared to enter the world. This does not mean that we need to stop inculcating and fostering good habits within our child/ren. What it does mean though, is that our input and influence are lessened due to their age. Interesting to note, the closer you are with your child the longer and more interested your child will be to your insights into their life. This is why it is vital to be loving and not strictly a disciplinarian.

CODDLING – PART II

One of the mistakes we discussed was coddling. We discussed how not to put down or argue with a teacher or a principal in front of the child as this will cause the authority figures at the school to be viewed as insignificant because daddy will set them straight.

The other coddling issue is where parents micromanage their kids. They get involved in everything that the child is doing so that the child feels stifled. I am not negating supervision at all, as being aware and involved is paramount. I am negating the overbearing parent who does not let their child breathe, figuratively speaking.

There are plenty of times where the parent must sit on the sidelines while their child figures it out for themselves. If you fight every battle for your child then this child will be unable to fight any battle without you. Of course, if a child is bullied in school or by a neighbor then you as the parent better get involved and stop the bully. What I am referring to, is a child who was not picked to be the lead part in the play. You as the parent must not fight this fight unless there is blatant nepotism such as six of the main parts have the same last name. Your job in this situation, in my humble opinion, is to hug him or her, wipe their tears and validate them. "You worked so hard. This must be so difficult for you. I feel your pain, etc."

Not once should you say, "This is malarky. I am going over to the theater director to give him a piece of my mind, etc.," as this is not helpful. A child must know that life ain't fair. A child must be taught that most times you will not be the chosen one. Most importantly, a child must learn humility.

CODDLING – PART III

Another type of coddling that can be a huge problem is spoiling your child. A healthy child must be taught at a young age to make their bed, bring the laundry to the laundry room, throw out their leftovers and put things away. These are just a few examples. Picking up after your child is unhealthy and will come back to bite you. If parents keep continue to spoil their child, they run the risk of having their child being diagnosed with, "spoiled child syndrome," which is characterized by the child being self-centered and immature which will culminate in unsavory behavior.

While it is true that we want to do so much for our kids, I need to tell you to stop doing that for your kids because you are doing more harm than good.

Of course, as parents, we do many things for them. We pack their backpacks when they are running late, we make their breakfast, lunch, dinner, and snacks every day. We run them to school when they miss the bus. We do these things just because we love them and we want them to know that. However, we also want them to learn how to be responsible for themselves. I personally know many families whose teenage kids have no idea how to stack and run the dish washer, let alone where the dishes go after being washed.

So, how on earth do you get them to pick up after themselves?

There are a few tricks to this trade.

1. Non-negotiable item — a clean room (add your own item here) is a must. Once they know that there is seriously no TV, Xbox or PlayStation they will get the message. I remember my kids in 7-11 wanted a candy bar and I told them that they cannot have it because we keep kosher. They stopped asking for the chocolate bar and started to point to the Twizzlers, which are kosher. I gave in.

2. Make sure that there is good music in the house when they are doing chores. This way they will bop to the beat as they are picking up the mess. It will go faster and easier with Billy Joel (add your favorite musician) in the background.

3. Make the kids focus on one chore at a time. Clothes first, then toys, then garbage pickup and then vacuum as an example.

4. Keep the toys organized. One box for cars and another for Legos and yet another for card games, etc.

KABBALISTIC INSIGHTS

There is a story told about a young couple who went to a Rabbi to settle their dispute. The mother wanted to send their toddler to a Jewish preschool while the father wanted to child to go to at 1ˢᵗ grade. The father argued that preschool is just basically a child sitting service.

The Rabbi inquired as to the age of their child. The couple responded 16 months. The Rabbi turned to them and he said "You are late in the game as a child's education begins at conception." Even when the child is in utero must we be careful what we say and do.

COMMON PARENTING MISTAKES III

LIFELONG LESSONS

I received an email, which I wholeheartedly agree with. The emailer took my lesson from Coddling II that advises parents not to fight your child's every battle and took it a step further. He wrote, "Failures at a young age are even better than successes. Successes everyone celebrates. They don't need us parents to celebrate. Of course, we do and that's great but that's not when we add value. We add value when they fail because it gives me the opportunity to teach them to accept it humbly and encourage them to get back up. Michael Jordan's saying about how many thousands of shots he missed and hundreds of games he lost in his life comes to mind here." Excellent point made by Frank H.

Moving away from coddling to parental expectations.

ACADEMIC PRESSURE

So many parents make the mistake of trying to advance their children beyond their years. My advice is to treat your child at his/her own age. Do not have expectations that are not age appropriate. As an example, and I hear this from parents often, "My child is three and can read fluently." I don't think that this is amazing. A 3-year-old needs to play, eat, make doo doo, sleep and try to fit puzzle shapes into the correct hole. If your child is three and can read fluently, then he/she has spent too much time being a 6-year-old and not a 3-year-old. Likewise, a 12-year-old child should be helping around the house, but he/she should not be the designated babysitter for the siblings or be responsible to prepare dinner. The 12-year-old should be enjoying life with some responsibility, but not as an indentured servant. My motto has always been "Let the kid be a kid."

Way too many parents push their kids so hard that it ends up having the opposite effect because of the immense pressure placed on them. The message a parent should place on a child is DO YOUR BEST and not BE THE BEST. Big difference. Do YOUR best is encouraging and positive while be THE best effects neurosis, causing the kid to twitch. As long as they do their best, you as a parent should be thrilled.

MARTYRDOM

As parents we never want to see our children fail or feel distress. Therefore, what we do is try and protect our child from difficult emotions. You work very hard to be sure he or she doesn't feel left out or frustrated. I remember working on one of my kid's their homework way more than they did. You want the road ahead to be as smooth as possible for your child. How can this be bad?

The problem is, when you rush in to do things for your child, what you're actually doing is sending a message that you don't think they're capable of handling the situation well on their own (even if it is true). You might be at your wits' end that they cannot do it. But the truth is—and this is important (see beginning of this article) — kids learn problem-solving skills as they fail. They learn to handle feelings of frustration only if they get to experience frustration. If you make the path too easy for your child, protecting them against every feeling of failure or frustration, you are keeping them from learning their own strength. And, you're exhausting yourself in the process!

Parents, stop working so hard. Allow your child to feel unhappiness or frustration. Of course, you as the parent need to find ways to help your child to manage those feelings. The barometer to check if you are a martyr is to ask yourself the following question, "Am I doing something that my child can really do for him or herself?"

The martyr mistake is not only common but very hard to diagnose. It usually takes an outsider, like a colleague or peer, to see it. We are subjective creatures in general, but even more so when it comes to our own kids. We can almost never see ourselves as a martyr, but rather, we view it as good parenting.

So, in addition to the advice given above, you need to seek counsel from a friend as to whether you should be up all night doing your child's homework or science project.

As a humorous anecdote, when any of my children did not do well enough on their science project to go to the next level, my wife and I use to slap each other high five and celebrate with a victory dance. One science project per year per child was more than enough for us. Exhausting.

Please feel free to share to all overworked, underappreciated martyr parents out there. Hopefully, a seed will be planted.

KABBALISTIC INSIGHTS

The Kabbala teaches us that we have two hands and arms. The right hand is for embracing, loving, giving and holding. The left however, is for pushing away and disciplining. We need both hands to rear children. A child must have loving contact with parents, while at the same time a child must be told no and never do this again.

You will notice that the right hand, which is traditionally the stronger hand is for love. Always show more love than disciple.

COMMON PARENTING MISTAKES IV

HANDLING PUNISHMENTS

We have been focusing on classic parental mistakes that every parent does with no exceptions. For the most part it has nothing to do with bad or poor parenting. On the contrary, because we seek to be good parents, we therefore feel the need to protect and shelter our kids with every fiber of our being. Unfortunately, due to our passion to be our children's savior, this can lead to errors.

So far, we have discussed Coddling, Martyrdom, and Criticism. Let's move on to other mistakes that are common and can be corrected just by being aware.

INCONSISTENCY

Inconsistent parenting is something that can cause your child to be able to manipulate you. A parent who constantly changes their mind or does not take a proper stand is likely to be bit by the manipulative kid bug. You see, our children are very intuitive and therefore easily pick up that a "no" does not necessarily mean a no, but rather, can also mean a "maybe." Teach them from an early age that a NO means an absolute, definitive and non-negotiable NO, unless you tell them from the onset that good behavior can change my mind.

As far as doling out punishments, do not make the mistake of boxing yourself into a corner by telling the kid that they will be punished by X,Y & Z. There is nothing worse than laying down the red line and not following through. If you tell them what consequences you are planning and then do not do it, you will have lost all credibility. They will be internally mocking you and you will lose respect for your parental authority.

The way to handle a punishment or consequence is to tell them that because of what they did there will be consequences. You need to think what those consequences will be and you will let them know. This way you are not boxed in and the kids know that there is a storm brewing in your mind. It will keep them on their toes. I learned this trick from my wife.

The real problem with parents who are unable to be firm is that it brings instability into the home. It is the children who will suffer because they too will also have instability, which can translate into wishy-washy values and morals, and lead to a weak personality. I once heard, and I wish I can remember where, that providing a stable home may not always be possible, but providing consistent parenting is always within reach. Up to us.

VALIDATION

I have to be honest. This is my kryptonite – right here.

When my children reveal their feelings and insecurities to me, I am quick to offer advice and counsel. I am smart enough to know that I should not contradict them or correct them. I do get into my unsolicited advice mode or I use it as an opportunity to talk about my experience in this regard. I have learned over the years, primarily as my kids got older and reminded me, to just listen and not talk.

Remember, they are taking a risk in opening up and involving you. All they want is to feel heard and understood, or in other words, they want to feel validated by their parents. They don't want a lecture, advice or your experience. What they want is your ear, heart and touch. After they finish opening up to you, give them a hug and thank them for trusting you. Their discussion may not require more than this, especially if they did not ask you a question. They just may need a safe place/person to talk to. Keep it safe and never ever criticize, as criticism is a very potent poison that causes alienation.

Of course, if they seek your advice, then give them adequate time to talk. If you do not have a good answer right then and there, tell them that you will digest what they asked you and you will get back to them in short order. Then pray.

As I said, the validation part took me awhile.

KABBALISTIC INSIGHTS

A home is a very special place. It must be a safe place where we can be vulnerable and feel loved at all times. In Judaism a home is called Mikdash Me'at – A Mini-Sanctuary. In other words, it is a holy place, just as the Big Temple in Jerusalem was holy.

The first event every morning in the Holy Temple was the consistent offering called the Tamid. The Tamid, which was offered every single morning before anything else was done. This teaches us that consistency and reliability are paramount.

GUIDING LIGHTS – HUMAN ANGELS

INSPRATIONAL PEOPLE – INSPIRED KIDS

Aside from fighting anti Semites, one of my other passions is trying to understand the parent and child dynamic. In my opinion, knowing how to navigate one's children at any age, takes skill, panache, Solomonic wisdom and a whole bunch of raw luck. I find it one of the most interesting and complex topics there is.

In a previous article I wrote that should always err on the side of compassion. I saw a great quote from Nelson Mandela that goes as follows "Our human compassion binds us the one to the other - not in pity or patronizingly, but as human beings." I think he sums it up pretty well.

In my thirst to learn more on this topic, I recently came across two stories of compassion that made my jaw drop. Parenthetically, I am an opportunist and whenever my jaw drops, I usually take advantage and eat a sandwich.

I will share the second story hopefully next article.

THE FIRST JAW DROP

This story is about Rabbi Moshe Feinstein, arguably one of the greatest Rabbis of the previous generation, venerated by so many, including yours truly, who studies his exegesis on Jewish law religiously. I actually met him once. A very formidable figure.

One summer he left the city for a month to study in the fresh country air in the Catskill Mountain to Camp Agudah, a sleep-away camp.

Rabbi Moishe Feinstein, even on vacation used to study many hours daily, often outside at a picnic table in the middle of camp. One day, in the midst of his study, he looks up and he sees in front of him a boy standing alone with nobody to play with. His bunk is off to somewhere, but not him, he was that kid that was left behind, the one that fell through the cracks of social norm play in his group of boys.

Rabbi Moishe Feinstein closes his book, gets up from the picnic table and walks up to this boy who's standing alone with no-one to play with, and he asks the boy, "Why are you alone? Why aren't you playing with the rest of your friends?"

And the boy looks up and says "I don't have any friends."

Rabbi Feinstein in his full garb with his tzitzit (fringes) flowing, bends down, picks up a ball and says to him, "Can I have a catch with you?" And he throws the ball to the boy and the boy throws the ball back to the great Rabbi Moshe Feinstein.

Do you get this? One of the greatest Jewish minds who ever lived was able to walk away from his study, which to him was vital as he was the world's foremost expert on contemporary Jewish law, and was able to close his books because he saw a kid that needed some help. He realized that this kid needed a friend to have a catch with.

If for Rabbi Moshe Feinstein it wasn't too lowly to show love to this kid, then what about us?

I believe the story captures the essence of compassion and I believe that it also teaches us the following vital lesson.

To be a good parent and/or teacher, you have to teach the child proper values and respect. To be a great parent/teacher in today's day and age, you need to be able to connect first and then teach later.

I think too many of us have forgotten this lesson and thanks to Rabbi Feinstein, I relearned the following. It is much easier to preach, yell, pontificate and orate than to stop working, bend down, pick up a ball and play catch. What this genius taught us by his actions was that ball playing is a much better teacher of respect than anything else.

KABBALISTIC INSIGHTS

Once, in the middle of the night, one of the second Lubavitch Rebbe's children fell out of bed. The Rebbe was in midst of study and he was so entirely absorbed in his studies, he did not hear the child's cries. However, the grandfather of the baby, the Alter Rebbe, heard the cries and went to see why the child is crying for so long.

The Alter Rebbe later said to his son, "no matter how deeply immersed you are Torah study, when a child cries you must hear it." Stop what you're doing and soothe their pain as this takes priority.

GUIDING LIGHTS – HUMAN ANGELS

INSPIRATIONAL PEOPLE – INSPIRED KIDS PART II

Last article I shared a phenomenal story of compassion where one of the greatest Jewish legal minds played a game of baseball catch with an 11-year-old boy who was socially inept.

I would like to share another story that brought me close to tears, as it captures humanity at its best. It teaches compassion, forethought and how as humans not to knee jerk react, something we are all familiar with. Admittedly, the hero in the following story makes compassion look easy, when in fact; it can be difficult to have consideration for someone who is driving you crazy. Nonetheless, it was an eye-opener for me to realize how far I still have to go in my "compassionate career" as a parent, husband, Rabbi, teacher and boss.

JAW DROPPING STORY #2

A young man turned to an elderly gentleman and said, "Hi Rabbi Cohen." Rabbi Cohen responded politely and asked genuinely, "With whom do I have the honor of speaking with?"

The young man replied, "30 years ago I was a student in your elementary class."

The older teacher replied, "Please remind me your name… oh yes I remember the name, and what do you do for a living?"

The young teacher replied, "Thanks to you, I too teach in an elementary Yeshiva."

"You teach because of me, how come?"

The young teacher replied, "I will remind the teacher of the story and you will understand.

'When I was a young boy, one of my classmates, who was not yet bar mitzvah, received an expensive watch. In those days, no one had a watch before they turned bar mitzvah. Only if they came from a wealthy family, they would receive a watch as a gift. All my classmates gathered around him to see the new watch. We were all jealous. During the break, the boy put the watch on his desk and when he returned, the watch had disappeared. Our teacher came to the classroom and told us that whoever took the watch must return it.

No one owned up.

So, the teacher told us to stand by the wall with our eyes closed and he checked our pockets one by one until he came to me and found the watch in my pocket. I was sure I would get expelled or some other big trouble, but to my surprise, he took the watch without anyone noticing, sat back in his chair, and said to the kids, 'I want you to know that the watch was not stolen; it was taken by one of the boys who is just struggling with issues. We have to give him the opportunity to fix what he did. This boy is not a thief and he is not a bad kid.'"

"This teacher was you," he continued.

"I was so relieved that you told everyone to close their eyes so they would not know it was me. I thought that later on you would take me to the side and give me hell for what I did. I waited for you to confront me, but as the days went by, you had not mentioned anything to me. Slowly, the incident was forgotten. The fact that you chose not to berate me made me even at such a young age want to pay it forward, so I too became an elementary school teacher.

"Do you remember the incident? Do you remember that it was me who took the watch?"

Old Rabbi Cohen replied, "No I do not remember."

"How come you do not remember? The teacher saw it was me!"

"I did not see," said Rabbi Cohen, "my eyes were also closed…"

I am completely in awe of this man's forethought and wisdom, and I aspire to be more like him when I grow up.

This is an educator. Someone who does not see the bad in his/her students, but rather, only the potential good. A great parent/teacher is someone who not only demands respect, but also gives respect.

KABBALSITIC INSIGHTS

The sixth Lubavitch Rebbe an essay on education where he expounded on what it takes to be a teacher.

The first step of an educator in his/her holy work, is introspection. A teacher must examine himself more earnestly and vigorously than a private individual.

An educator needs to review his method, to assure that it is deliberate and polite.

INSPIRATIONAL PARENTS – INSPIRED CHILDREN

Common sense and parenting do not necessarily go together. Proof of the pudding, you could have a parent who does everything right, yet the child fell far from the tree. Are we to blame the parents when we see a child acting out or being a hooligan? I personally do not think we can always say it is the parent's fault.

I bring proof from the Bible story of Rebecca and Isaac. They had two children – twins. Both boys were inculcated with the same principles and morals, but yet Jacob turned out righteous and Esau was corrupt to the core. Why is that? How can we explain this phenomenon?

One answer I can offer is something I learned while I was engaged to be married. I went to Montreal for a friend's wedding and I was there for a Shabbat and as a good young man, I went to a synagogue for services on a Saturday morning. I witnessed a father walk in from the hallway with literally eight boys all in a row. They sat down next to dad, opened their prayer book, and began reading. After services, I ran over to this man and I told him, "I am engaged and I plan on having a family and I wish to know your secret as to how all your children were so well behaved and inspired." He responded in a thick heavy Yiddish accent, "My secret? 10% discipline and 90% mazal – luck."

Wow. What a concept! His response was life altering for me. It allows me to acknowledge that, for the most part I am not in control of others. I am not the master of my children's destiny. Of course, this truth does not and cannot prevent me from doing my best. I absolutely need to teach my child right from wrong. There is a time when I need to compliment and there is a time to admonish. I may not abdicate my parental position of authority and just rely on luck, but rather, I need to be the best parent that I can be.

This leads me to the meaning of being a great parent. There are many facets to this. I wish to focus on just one for this current article.

BEING AN EXAMPLE

As a parent, you need to be a "living example" to your children. The kids are smart and they can see right through your baloney. If you are not sincere, they know it and sometimes even before you do. I am going to give an example that will resonate with my Jewish readers, but can be extrapolated to all.

Every parent wants to see their child "become" a Bar/Bat Mitzvah and read from the Torah from the dais, etc. It is SO important for their kid to do this. They drive them to the various appointments with the Rabbi or the Cantor and they pick out a nice suit, negotiate with the caterer and the DJ. They make sure that there are enough dancers for the party. Yet, the kids know for the most part that the parents did this for their ego and not due to religious/spiritual conviction. And once the celebration is over you will be hard pressed to see this newly minted Bar/Bat Mitzvah kid in Synagogue. He/she is like a bat out of hell.

What happened?

The parents were not inspired. They were truly excited, but not inspired. Their child did not see the parents go to prayer services just because they wanted to connect with God. They did not experience their father being enthused in prayer or their mother talking about Judaism. They heard a lot about Bar/Bat Mitzvah, but it was all fluff and airy and truly lacking substance.

So when a parent complains to me how can their child do this that or the other when he/she even had a Bar/Bat Mitzvah, I know exactly what transpired. Moms and dads: You want your kids to be inspired? You need to be inspired first. You cannot talk to your kid about respecting elders as a generic example when you do not respect elders. You need to SHOW them how it is done. Let them SEE firsthand your inspiration and then they will follow suit. While nothing is guaranteed in life, at least by being sincere you will have a chance. Never fall into the trap of do as I say, not as I do, as it does not work at all.

KABBALAH INSIGHTS

When the Kabbalah discusses the cosmic evolution, it speaks of four worlds. The lowest of the four is called "Asiya" which means action. Souls in physical bodies dwell in this world of action, and this is why most of the commandments contain physical items.

We need to act. We cannot expect our children to be enthused if we don't act. Words are meaningless if they are not backed by action.

TERRIBLE TEENS

A PARENTING TACTIC

We have all heard about the terrible twos where a toddler gets into everything and everywhere. I remember those days. The complete destruction of tissue boxes and the pure joy at throwing food on the floor. I also can recollect the temper tantrums. As 98% of all parents can attest, the worst ones were held either in a supermarket or at a restaurant. I deliberate whether I still have PTSD – Post Toddler Stress Disorder. I think I have developed a restaurant phobia and a ShopRite twitch.

However, nothing compares to the other PTSD, i.e., Post Teenager Stress Disorder. This is a real-life makeover. As a mom of teenagers Yvette Manes writes, "I thought that raising teenagers would be like those goofy old Brady Bunch episodes about curfews, acne and dating. It is not. It is more like Survivor meets Dateline." Teenagers are highly emotional, extremely irrational, exceedingly hungry and exceptionally rude. I know, I know, not your teenager but definitely most. As a father of teenagers, I have reached the stage of parenthood where I have taken to watching Rosemary's Baby for comfort!

There is one question that all parents have, "Why do they act like this?" Then there is the second more important question, "What on earth can we do about it?"

As to the why they act like this, I will leave it to the experts to try and figure out the teenage brain. The short answer that I have come up with is that they are a work in progress. I use the dough analogy when describing a teenager. When a dough is half-baked, it is neither dough nor bread. It is this hybrid between the two. A teenager is neither a child nor an adult, but rather a warm gooey mess whose brain needs some more time to harden.

I do have some thoughts though as to what we can do about it, or at the very least, how to minimize the dysfunction that causes so much upheaval in one's home due to the volatility of the post-pubescent youth.

You see, teenagers build a wall between adults and themselves. They view parents, teachers and any other form of authority as the enemy. They feel judged and belittled by the slightest criticism. In extreme cases, they cannot even stand the sound of their parents' voices, even if the parents are talking about something good. So, they tune the parents out. Familiar with this behavior?

They loath therapists as they feel that the parents make them go to a person whom the enemy is paying to sabotage and control them. The bottom line: the wall goes higher and gets thicker with every dollar we give them and with every word that is emitted from our heavily caffeinated mouths.

How does one break down the barriers between you and your teen? The tried and proven method is to love and connect with them. Arguing and criticizing are poison and will cause this bit of dough to remain uncooked or worse, it will get moldy.

What my wife and I have learned from others is to bombard them with compliments and shower them with praises. Even if your child does something small to help clean the house, make sure that you make a big deal out of it, but not in a cheesy way. Celebrate their B minus as if they got an A+. Make them feel valued, cherished and so important that their self-esteem rises. Just as in the bread baking analogy, if you fail to add yeast the bread will be flat and tasteless. So too when a child is raised without self-esteem, he or she will be lackluster and feel flat, which in turn will make them angry, rude and dysfunctional.

Love is the antidote – the medicine.

There is a great story about Rabbi Yisroel Belsky. He passed away in 2016. You can google him as he held many titles and accomplished much in his lifetime. The story goes like this.

He was asked, "What is it that your mother did that enabled you to become the great man, scholar, Rabbi you are today?" Questions like "Did she pray for you all day long?" His answer was "My mother would hold me and sing to me, 'You are my sunshine, my only sunshine…'" He said that when she sang that to him, it made him feel very beloved and that he could accomplish anything.

Add a little sunshine and warmth to the dough and it will be a healthy batch.

When we infuse our child(ren) with love and tell them that we believe in them, they will become stable and great and make us proud.

KABBALAH OF TEENAGERS

When our children are young, all they have is their parents and family. They look up to us, they heavily rely on us and they often copy our sayings and mannerisms. They are receiving our light. They do not have their own light yet. They are like a moon.

When a child grows, he or she start offering some of their own light. They are becoming less moon and more sun.

It is the transition from moon to sun that makes them that makes them shaky. Once the change is over, they then (hopefully) return to being sweet and amicable.

HOW TO TACKLE YOUR CHILD'S FOLLY

I saw a meme the other day and it made me literally stop what I was doing (probably eating something) and I thought to myself, OMG this is brilliant. The very same meme led me to writing the following thoughts.

The meme went something like this, "If you have told a child a thousand times and he/she still does not understand, then it is not the child who is the slow learner." Boom! What an incredible and true thought.

So. Let us process this.

If you have a child who does something wrong time and time again, and you give them a piece of your mind again and again, and the child does not change their behavior, then it is high time for you to change yours.

Bear in mind that if your child does get the message and listens to you after two to three times, then you are in great shape, and you need to read no further and give me a call because I need advice.

What to do with a child who does not change even when you yell, shout, rebuke, threaten and punish?

I believe that there are three responses, and they do not include criticizing or penalizing. In fact, any child who is a repeat offender will suffer severe "damage to the spirit" if we keep on at them over and over. And the more spirit damage, the more trouble they will get into, and feel unworthy and despised, causing them to act out further, and on and on and on. A terrible and futile strategy.

So, what to do?

I believe that there are three responses to a child who is recalcitrant. (Notice I did not say recalcitrant child). Before we get to them, there is something fundamental that needs to be understood. THIS CHILD IS IN PAIN. This is the reason as to why he/she cannot get their act together, whether at home or in school. A truly bad egg is a true rarity. This child is not bad, just in a lot of pain.

Here it goes.

The first response is to say nothing. No yelling. No chiding. No logical lectures. No pleading. Nothing. You realize that this child is hurting and you do not want to damage the spirit further. So, you simply let it go without scolding, as you would if your child was in great physical pain.

71

The second is to say nothing at the time of infraction because of the heat of the moment. Let 24 hours lapse so that you can calm down and address the transgression with a cool head, without any rancor or belittling. You can talk to your child as you would address your spouse (eh. scratch that) or another person with explanations as to what the expectations are.

The last choice, and by far the most difficult, is to simply grin and bear it and address it with levity. However, do not forget the grin part. Remember, this approach takes an incredible amount of strength. You see, the weak yell, but the strong think. If you berate this kid, you will cause damage. If your child in pain does something wrong, the best response is to put your arm around him/her with one hand and tousle his/her hair with the other and tell them that you love them and there is not a thing in the world that will come between them and your love.

As example: You find your child smoking in the police precinct. Tell your child lovingly with a smile that they are crazy for smoking in a police station right under the no smoking sign. If you yell at them for smoking then what separates you from the cops in the room? You are not a cop, you are his/her mom.

I once heard advice from a wise man that if you ever reach a point where you cannot stand your kid due to bad behavior, then go into a room where there is a cute picture of him or her and fall in love all over again.

By doing this third method you will not only NOT damage their spirit, but rather, they will feel loved, worthy, upbeat and it will translate into healing their broken spirit, which in turn, will curb some of their bad behavior, which was all part of a self-fulfilling prophecy in the first place. I have witnessed first-hand people who practice the third way, and while it is truly difficult to grit their teeth into a smile, it does eventually get easier to do because their child got easier to handle.

Please share this short but important message with any parent who is struggling. Aren't we all? May the force of parenting be with you.

KABBALISTIC INSIGHTS

The holy and mystical of Tanya quotes the Arizal, Rabbi Isaac Luria, that anger must be avoided at all costs because essentially, if one gets angry at something or someone, he or she is denying the hand of God in his or her life.

PERMISSIVE, OVERBEARING & BROADMINDED

THE THREE ATTITUDES OF PARENTING

I am a realist, and I know that I made many mistakes, blunders and slip-ups while rearing my children, and still do. To my credit, I have apologized to my kids and have owned up to my missteps.

I am putting pen to paper for a few reasons. The main two would be to help someone else avoid the errors I made, and secondly, to teach, which as a Rabbi is my primary responsibility, the Jewish view and attitude of parenting.

The reason as to why there are different types of parents is that there are different types of emotive attributes that we have been endowed with. The Kabbalah teaches us that there are three primary emotional faculties that we possess, Chessed, Gevurah and Tiferet, which are loosely translated into Giving, Restricting and Compassion. The other way to translate this is Kindness, Severity and Harmony.

When a parent/teacher/manager has an imbalance of Chessed then they will be especially kind, forgiving and tolerant. Sounds good – no? The Kabbalah tells us though that this is not the way to be because a child or student who never hears "no" will grow up to be narcissistic, egomaniacal, self-absorbed and selfish. Every child needs to be disciplined and be told that their poor behavior will not be tolerated. One can argue that NYC under Mayor Koch had too much Chessed and hooligans were in control and justice was pitifully weak.

On the flip side of the same coin, if you are a parent who is very strict and overbearing, it is because of the imbalance of Gevurah in your system which the Kabbalah says is not good either. The child will be stifled and may grow up to not be self-sufficient, or worse, possess a complete inability to have a fully functioning life.

The good news is that even if you are born with an imbalance, you have the complete power in your control to fix it. All you need to do is be aware of this disparity and then lean to the other side to overcome it. In other words, if you are too permissive with your child, you need to be aware and act accordingly. One idea that has worked for me is this. When I am asked for something completely irrational or unacceptable from one of my children, instead of answering right away, I will respond that I need to think about it. This assures that I can think it through with a clear and balanced mind.

The best approach says the Kabbalah is Tiferes, which is compassion. One needs to ask themselves when dealing with their underling the following, "Is this response compassionate or not?" Forget about giving too much or taking away. Just focus on compassion.

I have often used this example by way of illustration. Once when I was engaged to be married, I was on the phone with my fiancé who is now my wife. She lived on the West Coast and I on the East. Since we were engaged and infatuated, we spoke for many hours into the early morning. Was this five-hour-long chat Chessed or Gevurah? On the one hand, it was beautiful pleasantries in which we exchanged our mutual love. On the other hand, she had to teach kindergarteners in a couple of hours while I could sleep in. She would be exhausted and it was so unfair to keep her on the phone. So was my beautiful phone call that I initiated kindness or severity?

While I do not know the answer to this question, I could tell you this, if I thought about being compassionate during this phone call, I would have told her that she needs her beauty sleep and that I will talk to her the next day. The bottom line is this. Always err on the side of compassion and let it be your guiding light.

KABBALISTIC INSIGHTS

The Kabbalah explains that Tiferes (harmony/compassion) is comprised of Chessesd (kindness) and Gevurah (severity). As explained above Chessed alone has flaws. Gevurah by itself has flaws. It is only when they both fuse together can harmony and compassion find expression.

BREAD OF SHAME – A LESSON IN PARENTING

There is a fascinating lesson that the Kabbalah teaches with regards to the story of Adam & Eve eating of the forbidden fruit. To me, this is the lesson of all lessons and one that is often ignored by parents of millennials.

As you may know, Adam & Eve were introduced to the Garden of Eden and were told "You may eat from every tree, except this one in the middle." Can you imagine being Adam & Eve? You had every available fruit and veggie at your disposal, all organic, non GMO and wax free to boot, so many of them being exotic and colorful, yet you eat the ONLY one that you were told not to eat!! Insane!! Enjoy the grapes, dates, oranges, mangos, papaya and eat as many as you want at no charge. Just leave the one single solitary tree alone as this is all God asks of you. Yet, you go ahead and defy God, who immediately kicks you out of the Garden where now you have to fend for yourself. What is wrong with you anyway?

The Kabballah comments and calls this "Bread of Shame."

Bread of Shame is what Adam & Eve felt when every single one of their needs and whims were met without earning it, without working for it. This feeling of unworthiness eventually led to resentment of God which led to an attitude like who is He to tell us that we cannot eat this particular fruit? We don't care what He says and we will do what we want, when we want, and how we want.

It is fascinating to read the punishment Adam & Eve received. They had to WORK for their food. The Torah/Bible tells us that God told them that from now on they would have to plow, sow and reap. No more freebies. No more mango sorbet or kale smoothies on demand.

This is a quintessential parenting lesson.

Our children, even older ones, will feel the Bread of Shame if we continue spoiling them. They will feel unworthy if their every need, whim and impulse is met on a silver platter, not unlike Adam & Eve. A child or any human being for that matter, need to feel like they earned it. Statistics show that lottery winners usually end up broke and bereft of any savings. You know why? They did not earn this moncy, so they abuse it and have no respect or regard for it.

The practical solution to ensure that our children do not feel worthless, entitled or feel any bread of shame is to assure that they earn their keep. From an early age, give them chores around the house. Make sure that they do not receive allowance from you when their room is a mess or they have not done a stitch of homework. Keep them honest. Just giving them money because they are your kid is a mistake, as they will end up resenting you.

As they get older, the stakes get higher.

As an example, do not, under any circumstances, buy your child a car without them putting in serious money from their savings and/or babysitting account. If you buy them a car (new or used) with no sacrifice on their part, they will not treat their car with respect. Never buy them the latest and the greatest car either, even with their financial input, as this is equally unhealthy. My suggestion is to start them off with a small and safe car — nothing too big or grandiose.

Lastly, there is a message for teachers as well. Do not give the student an A on their report because you do not wish to deal with a difficult parent. This will only end up hurting the child when he/she goes into the real world. Let them learn consequences of not studying. Let them learn that they cannot excel at everything.

KABBALISTIC INSIGHTS

The Mishna states "Love work." Going to work is healthy. It is not only good for one's self worth, it is also allows us to do what we were created for. Human beings are the only creation that can elevate something physical to holiness. As an example, when we give some of our hard-earned money to charity, one's entire work week becomes a holy enterprise and not just a means to an end.

UNIQUE SOULS

A PARENT'S GUIDE TO REARING CHILDREN

A few years ago, a dear friend of mine, Levi Deitsch, lost his father due to a heart operation that was not successful. His father did something remarkable before going under the knife. He wrote an individual letter to every one of his children in case he did not recover from the surgery. Levi told me that it was so helpful to him that his father did this and that he too plans to write a letter to his children.

A few years later, Levi was stricken with lung cancer and I reminded him of our conversation. He told me that he already has plans to record a unique mini movie by simply having someone film him. He was unable to write, but he made his impression to his children before he passed. His beautiful children have loving images of their father with them, each being named individually.

I think that there are two life lessons to be gleaned from this sad story.

One is that we need to let our children know how much we love them and not just posthumously or close to that time, but at every opportunity we can.

Secondly, our love has to be unique to each separate child. Levi's father, Zalman of blessed memory, did not write the exact same letter to each child, but rather, he penned separate thoughts and emotions to each one of his kids. Levi did not record one single video to his kids, but rather took the time in his very sickly state to talk to his kids individually. Zalman and Levi both could have conveyed their love in a single letter or recording but chose to connect on a completely different level as each child is a unique soul and therefore a different kind of bonding needs to take place.

I once heard a story which made a great impact on me. Someone complained to her Rabbi that one of her kids was acting inappropriately. She bemoaned that she does not understand how this could be as all her children were brought up exactly the same, with the same rules, dinners and expectations. The Rabbi responded that this was a gross error. He said, "You cannot bring up all your children the same as they are not robots or carbon copies. Each child needs to be brought up differently."

The Kabballah teaches us that we are all created with different strengths and we need to hone in and work them through. To try to be someone else is foolish and to try to force someone to be like someone else is criminal. The Kabballah cites an example that Rabbi Hillel was a very lenient Rabbi and he always saw the cup half-full. This is because he was created with a high-level dose of Chessed – kindness or compassion. To change his personality would have meant that his scholarly works of which Jewish law relies on today would have been lost or curtailed.

A parent must realize this truism. Accept the child for what he or she is and do not try to fit them in our narrow vision of what your child should be or not be for that matter. Teach them good values and then let them soar to great heights.

KABBALISTIC INSIGHTS

Just as there are no two fingerprints alike, there are no two people created for the same purpose. God did not create redundancy. Just as each person has a unique DNA code embedded in them, so too, each human being has a mission to complete that is completely different than someone else.

A SLAP AND A KISS

A PARENTING STRATEGY

Unless I have selective amnesia, I believe that I was a decent son and student growing up. I studied assiduously, completed my class and homework on time and was pretty well behaved at home and in school most of the time.

I remember during one end of the spring hot and humid day, when most kids (globally) were not in the mood of school and teachers, I too acted out and was being somewhat boisterous and to my chagrin the teacher called my house to let them know that I was a terror in school. I do not remember what the specific transgression was but it was clearly enough to warrant a call from a teacher. When I got home my father told me that Rabbi Sufrin had called to let him know of my wrongdoings. He told me that he was disappointed in me and why would I act out like that. He told me not to follow bad examples, blah blah blah.

He then said something to me that I believe to be one of the most brilliant things I have ever heard. He said these magical words. "It was not becoming of me to behave like this." This is what I call a slap and a kiss. With this very phrase, he put me down and he raised me up simultaneously. You see, what he was doing was conveying his disappointment, while simultaneously telling me I was better than this. He let me know that he knows I am better and that I should know it too. He was telling me to get my stuff together and be my better self. Brilliance.

The above anecdote reminds me of something I learned early on in my Yeshiva days. The Kabballah teaches us that God created us with two hands. The right hand belongs to the realm of kindness and the left to world of discipline. Our right hand which is the dominant one is used to embrace while the left, which is weaker, is used to push away or discipline.

A parent must always display their strong love to their children, and once in a while, a parent must discipline. The telling off or the punishment must never be as strong as the love and must always fit the crime. Otherwise, the punishment is more about you venting instead of this being a teachable moment for the child. The ideal is when the right and left hand, the love and discipline come together in a perfect embrace. Telling a child that it is not becoming of him / her is the perfect blend.

Another example of a perfect blended slap and a kiss. When your child comes home from school and you have just received the report card. If it mainly A's and B's then obviously the right hand comes out with a caress and a tussle of the hair followed by a kiss. But what if the report card is C's and D's?

I believe that a healthy child probably feels bad enough without the parent reprimanding them. My suggestion is to tell them that "We believe in you and we know that you can do better next time and we will help because we love you." Never ever tell them that you are disappointed in them but rather seize the moment to get a tutor and call the school. And no, never get them an algebra book for a birthday or Chanukah present.

Interesting to note the same Kabalistic teaching mentioned earlier is of the opinion is that mankind is the microcosm of the world at large. Meaning that all of this world operates in the same way. There needs to be a perfect balance and blend of Chessed which is kindness and Gevurah which is discipline in order for the world to function at its peak.

Too much kindness without severity or discipline will lead to lawless society where the criminals are not afraid of anything like in the movie Goodfellas. Too much severity not tempered by kindness leads to world wars and genocide.

Now go find your balance.

KABBALISTIC INSIGHTS

Balance is the answer.

In life we need balance. A workaholic who never sees his family is out of balance, while the same is true of an idle soul who is also out of balance. The same is true of everything else that we encounter. A balanced life is rewarding.

EGOLESS PARENTING

THE PROPER APPROACH

I recently wrote about anger and how counterproductive it actually is. At the time one is angry, he/she is not thinking about how to best resolve the crisis, but rather, is focused on themselves and how hurt they are.

The problem with unbridled anger is that it is considered worshipping the self and has no real merit. The same would be true with any egocentric attribute such as arrogance or self-importance. There is simply not enough room to think about others. Someone I respect once told me that ego is an acronym for "Easing God Out." Since the egotistical person mainly thinks of himself, it is axiomatic that he is not thinking about God either.

Let us bring this home to parenting.

Let's be honest. A child can survive without a teacher. A child can survive without a principal. A child can survive without a coach, massage, yoga instructor, sensei or driver's Ed. What a child needs more than anything else in the world, at least in the formative years, is a parent, and if the parent is not selfless to the child, then the child will suffer.

Therefore, if/when a child does something wrong and the auto reflex of a parent is to get upset at their child, at this very critical moment, the parent needs to analyze whether their response is selfish or selfless. You see, a selfish parent is thinking about themselves. I did not bring you up this way and therefore you have failed me or our family's reputation. What will cousin Ida think or what will the neighbors think will create a response in one way, while a selfless parent will respond in another.

A selfish parent will scold their child whose actions are perfidious and bring embarrassment to the family. In other words, being embarrassed by your child is more important than your child. The thought is that the child needs to go away to a boarding school or another institution because "We can't take it anymore." Whereas a selfless parent will ask the child, "What is ailing you? What can I do to help you?"

You see the difference? One response is oy vey to me and the other response does not mention me, but rather mentions the welfare of the child, as in how can I help you. Huge difference.

Recently, I was called a hypocrite because my child did not act in accord with my values. Yet, I still embraced this child as if nothing happened. I would agree with the individual that I am a hypocrite if I acted in opposing my morals and values. However, this was not about me. This was about my child. For me it was contrary to my value system, but for this child it was not.

We have about 15 to 16 years to really make an impact on our kids. After that, they are getting ready to fly the coop and see the large yonder. Nine out of ten times a child will be different than their parents and we need to not stoke the fires of conflict as this is the fires of the burning ego. Rather, we need to find common ground so that the family remains intact and wholesome.

It takes an incredible amount of strength to love one's child even though they are acting out. And it takes incredible weakness to lash out at them when "you" feel hurt by them.

Always keep this following thought before a negative interaction with your child.

Am I angry because of how it affects me or am I concerned about my child? If it is about you then go take a bath with sachets of lavender. However, if it is about how your child is doing, then plaster on a smile and make loving contract.

KABBALISTIC INSIGHTS

I heard a story once that there were two yeshiva administrators looking at a yellow school bus that was for sale. The Lubavitcher Rebbe walked by and asked them what they were gazing at. They responded "this bus is for sale, and we are thinking about purchasing it."

The Rebbe looked at the bus and told them "this bus is a jalopy." The administrators responded "this is all they can afford."

The Rebbe was incredulous and he responded. "You know why you can't afford the money for a new bus? Because in your mind, the old and run-down bus will suffice for your yeshiva."

While a person should not have an inflated ego, they should never forget their self-worth and the self-worth of those around them.

POLITICS

ELECTIONS

A RABBI'S REFLECTION

Let's face it, we're smack in the middle of a time where we need to make some tough choices.

The decisions we will make in the coming days may be some of the most consequential of our lifetime.

So much is at stake, and we need to be the ones to make the right decision for this moment, whilst recognizing the reality of the impact our decisions might have for years to come.

Further, we know those choices aren't easy. Americans just like you and me are grappling with these tough calls right now, and are sitting at home poring over research, wondering whom do I vote for. It is not just the presidency, but also many other local and non-local races.

Such anxiety, angst and worry…

WHOM TO VOTE FOR

I asked myself what helpful advice can I offer as a Rabbi without getting into the very muddy and turbulent waters of politics. Truth be told, no Rabbi should ever tell you for whom you must vote, as it is simply unfair. While you may have read that this group of Rabbis support Trump for President and this group of Rabbis endorse Biden, it is wrong, plain and simple. If we have learned nothing else from this pandemic, it is humility. Look how little we know about the coronavirus, let alone anything else. While I will always defer to great Rabbis, I do not want them to tell me who to vote for as it takes away my free will, which was given to me as a gift from above.

I readily admit that I am somewhat guilty of the above. While I have never told anyone who to vote for, I have been outspoken unnecessarily on politics. What I mean by "unnecessarily" is offering my opinion on something political, like who is moral and who is immoral, and who will go down in history as a good or horrible politician. I have thankfully learned to keep my opinion to myself.

Having said the above, I will always stand up to anti-Semitism. I will go toe to toe with a member of congress, governor or even a president, and I will do so vociferously. I know (not just think) that we have to be constantly vigilant when it comes to anti-Semitism.

MY HUMBLE OFFERINGS

So what advice, counsel, guidance and direction can I offer you that will be helpful and take away some of the torment we are all going through?

FOUNDING PRINCIPLE

Among the founding principles in Judaism are Emunah (faith) and Bitachon (trust). To distinguish between the two, Emunah is that there is a God and He forges my destiny and fate. No human being, even an extremely powerful one, can change what God has decreed for me. While it is true that I have free will, this is only in moral decisions that I make.

Bitachon means trust. God wants what is good for me. While I am responsible to be proactive and hands on, I am not in charge of the outcome and I definitely am not the arbitrator of the results. While I do my part and I go to work, I rely and trust heavily on God. In the words of the Psalmist, "I cast my burdens and place it on God."

GO VOTE! ANOTHER PRINCIPLE

Therefore, when I vote on Election Day (or before), I am doing my part, but I will completely put my trust, faith, hope and reliance on God. The obvious question that comes to mind is if God is in control then why even bother to vote. The answer to this leads me into another great principle of Judaism. One cannot simply go about life asking God to take care of them without effort from the individual. One cannot expect to win the lottery if one does not buy a lottery ticket. We have to do our part. We must vote and then let God do His part.

BE HUMBLE

In these final few days before the election, I ask you to not only go vote but also be humble. Respect someone else's point of view even if it is baffling and feels wrong. I also ask you to pray for the best outcome for our country.

In conclusion, regardless of the outcome of your decision-making process and the results of the election, I very much hope to be able to share many good times together with you in the future days where COVID-19 is a distant, yet sore, memory.

Wishing you the very best of luck in all the tough choices you need to make.

KABBALISTIC INSIGHTS

Angels do not have free will. They do as they are told and are always reacting to God's instructions. Humans on the other hand have free will and are the only creation in the entire universe that has the ability to trespass God's will and instruction.

A great reward awaits those who suppress a desire to do something improper because God says so.

A POST ON POST ELECTION

WHERE DO WE GO FROM HERE

I know I speak for many when I say whew! Thank the good L-rd that November 3rd has passed and the election is now over. While it is true that the results of the Presidential election may take a while due to the closeness of the count, it is nonetheless over. The relentless campaigning is over. The radio and TV advertisements can now go back to auto insurance and laundry detergents. This has been a long election cycle and we have had enough.

Of course, the dark cloud of the outcome will be fought in court battles and the animosity will continue for a short while, but for the most part, we the people have spoken. Though it remains to be seen what the courts think we have said.

We are now after the elections and if you are like me, you have freed up about 50 billion neurons and 400 billion glial. What should I do with all the brain space that I now have? Can you imagine if you were a laptop? You would have so much more room for useless GIFs.

Psychology as well as applied Kabbalah teaches that empty minds lead one to empty or even worse debased thoughts, which will lead someone down to the moral abyss. Therefore, we need to take this newfound space and quickly fill it with something worthwhile.

My humble suggestions are as follows:

DO & DON'TS

DO turn off the radio and TV and swear off the politics for a while. It is done and over. The vitriol and venom being spewed is not healthy. Do as I do and take a well-deserved break. It is time to heal.

DO apologize to anyone you may have hurt in the heat of an argument. Ask yourself, was it worth it? Did you change their mind? Did they change your mind? Does it pay to still have the bad feelings and bad energy wafting around the atmosphere?

DO take some of the free brain space you now have and use it to read up on a self-help book or a book on spirituality. After this election cycle (and the last for that matter), we need to spend time on self-improvement. There are plenty of books that I can recommend.

DO volunteer and do something worthwhile. Our country is blessed because it is built on kindness and compassion. We must never lose these noble traits. While many of us have been preoccupied, it is now time to go back to basics. Help is sorely needed.

DON'T go around gloating if your candidate/s won their election. You had one vote among many and it is not yours to triumph. You can and should be happy but not revel in someone's face. After all, the candidate is not yours per se but rather ours. Instead, pray that he or she does the right thing for the constituents.

DON'T despair if the candidate you voted for lost their election. It was clearly not the people's will and undoubtedly not God's will either. You will survive. You do not have to run to Canada out of fear. Maybe a trip to Bali will do you good though. There are a few anti-Semitic candidates that I wish were voted out; I am not going to fret and shake in my boots that they were reelected. I am going to stand up to them if they continue along their previous noxious past. I won't be silenced and I will not fret.

Having said the above, I will always tell my fellow Jews (no matter which country) who have repeatedly been the catalyst of much hate to always have unexpired passports ready. It was smart in Germany, France and the rest of Europe back then. It is prudent now. Jews have always been canaries in the coalmine. Unfortunately, the attacks start with Jews, but do not end exclusively with us. Even recent history has taught this perilous lesson. Hopefully, we will not have to flee anytime soon. Just be prepared. This is especially true for the Jews in France.

DON'T knock democracy. It works and it is extremely powerful. While nothing is perfect, it is the closest thing we have to perfection. Of course, things can be tweaked here and there and they should be and hopefully will be, but it is far better than what else is out there. I am always awed by both the wisdom and humility of the Founding Fathers. You can tell that they were steeped in faith and were absolutely open to change.

I apologize if I offended anyone during the heat of the moment. Humanity is a work in progress.

KABBALISTIC INSIGHTS

The holy book of Zohar states "When man accomplishes G-d's will below, he causes a parallel rectification above." This is an amazing line. G-d created the world in such a way where our thoughts, speech and actions are felt in the upper worlds.

ARE WE TOO SENSITIVE?

WATERSHED MOMENTS

There are certain pivotal moments that we witness or are a part of, that are so incredibly auspicious and or life altering that we simply can never forget that they happened. Most of these events are very individual like the day you get married or the moment you become a parent. Some of them however happen at the world at large and you say to yourself "holy moly" did I just witness history being made? Or did this just happen during my lifetime?

You know what I mean. We all know exactly where we were and what we were doing and thinking when we learned that the first plane that hit the twin tower on 9/11 was not a pilot error but a terrorist attack on the eastern shores of these United States. Landing on the moon, Kennedy assassinations, the Iran hostage debacle, gay marriage becoming legalized, etc. All these were watershed moments.

Sadly, we have been witness to another watershed moment that will "live in infamy" and can never be erased from the history books. I am not talking about the spewing of classic anti Semitic by a congresswoman but rather the response or lack thereof by the leaders of our country.

First, let's address a question that many people including fellow Jews and members of congress are asking.

Are we the people simply too sensitive? What is the big deal? Someone in Congress, a newbie at that, puts their foot in their mouth and all of a sudden it becomes a national argument pitting people against one another. Let it go? We have so many more important things to discuss like global terrorism, global economy, equal rights, North Korea and Brexit. Who needs to get so crazed over one individual who is still in the learning curve of diplomacy? And by the way, this same verbal offender had a tough and rough upbringing in the upheaval of Mogadishu. Let it go and let's move on.

Furthermore, no one got killed, no one got maimed. You can't compare this to the Pittsburgh Synagogue massacre where 11 Jews were killed by a white supremist. I mean just this week there were swastikas drawn in a Long Island synagogue. It is this hate that we need to eradicate not free speech.

Yup, I had these thoughts and questions too.

Here is the truth of the matter and this is why it is bad not only for Jews in this country but for all moral and upstanding citizens of this great Republic.

You see when an anti Semitic act occurs and the police respond and catch the perp, or even if they do not catch the fool, there is a certain confidence that this is an heinous act and everyone in authority agrees that this must not be tolerated and that someone cares. Point in fact when the Pittsburgh massacre occurred by a white Nazi supremist animal in human form, the President of the United States came to the place of horror and condemned it. He clearly stated that this is not ok and in essence telling the Jews and the aforementioned good people that we got your back.

Furthermore, these goons who commit these acts whether swastikas and or cross burnings while truly evil are punks who probably should be in prison for 20 to 30 other crimes against humanity. They are buffoons. Even the fancy ones like David Duke in a shirt, suit and a tie is still a thug in a suit as opposed to a thug wearing jeans or spandex.

However, when a member of Congress who is the elite of the elite of our nation, who was elected by thousands upon thousands of people spews her garbage on a constant basis (at least every two weeks) then there is a huge problem.

Then you add insult to injury, salt on a wound, sugar in the insulin, fuel to the fire, carbon monoxide in the oxygen tank by the very fact that the rest of the elite of the elite, the Congress as a body firstly refusing to condemn this politician by name and then watering it down by condemning all sorts of nastiness. This is a watershed moment. True, there were isolated members of Congress who denounced her. They did in fact stand up and do the right thing but it not a condemnation that was befitting our leaders of this great Republic.

How on earth did things get so far so fast? I say who cares.

It was a shameful moment. It is a blight on our countries record and it can never be erased. This stain is here to stay.

Should we Jews and other moral, good and upright be nervous about what occurred? Yes. Once again this was a watershed moment because anti Semitism was given a free pass by the very leaders who were elected whose sole mission is to protect their citizens.

KABBALISTIC INSIGHTS

We learn from the few Biblical verses dedicated to Matzah, the poor man's bread, that there are two types of humility.

Matzah, unlike bread has no yeast so therefore does not rise. These teaches us that we need to rid ourselves of ego, inflated pride and arrogance.

The other lesson of matzah is that it was made with haste and it did not have time to rise. We need to move with alacrity at all times. The fact that Congress dragged its feet in condemning anti Semitism is concerning. We know from our own lives when we do not want to do something, we put it on the back burner.

Perhaps Congress should serve matzah, a little humility in their sacred halls.

AN IMPORTANT SUPREME COURT RULING

THE RULING

Last week the Supreme Court made its voice heard in favor of the Diocese of Brooklyn and the Orthodox Agudath Israel of America, who have churches and synagogues in areas of Brooklyn and Queens, and who have at one time or another been designated as red and orange zones. In red and orange zones, the state capped attendance at houses of worship at 10 and 25 people, respectively.

The justices acted on an emergency basis, temporarily barring New York from enforcing the restrictions against the groups while their lawsuits continue. In an unsigned opinion, the court said the restrictions "single out houses of worship for especially harsh treatment."

"Members of this Court are not public health experts, and we should respect the judgment of those with special expertise and responsibility in this area. But even in a pandemic, the Constitution cannot be put away and forgotten. The restrictions at issue here, by effectively barring many from attending religious services, strike at the very heart of the First Amendment's guarantee of religious liberty," the opinion said.

THE GOVERNOR

While I am not personally a big fan of the Governor, I do believe that he does care for his State and that he legitimately feels tremendous concern and is rightfully scared for the people under his jurisdiction. Having said the above, our Governor (like someone else from Queens we know) was not so happy when the ruling came down, and he dismissed it as irrelevant as there are currently no restrictions in place.

Instead of hearing their wisdom, he, in his unqualified manner, simply dismissed it as politics. He opined that the new Supreme Court just wants to make a political point.

Not so fast Governor.

AN INCREDIBLE RULING

The Supreme Court's ruling was anything but irrelevant. It was fundamental and especially so if he is considering another lockdown, which he has hinted at doing.

To me the most important opinion came from Justice Gorsuch where he wrote in support of the court's decision. He noted that while Cuomo's executive order arbitrarily limited church attendance in COVID hotspots to 10 or 25 people, it put no such restrictions on liquor stores, bike shops, acupuncturists, accountants and other supposedly "essential" businesses.

Gorsuch also wrote, "So, at least according to the Governor, it may be unsafe to go to church, but it is always fine to pick up another bottle of wine, shop for a new bike, or spend the afternoon exploring your distal points and meridians."

SELECTIVE DISCRIMINATION

If you were around New York City and Long Island, for the strict Coronavirus lockdowns imposed earlier this year, you totally understand what Gorsuch meant. Many of us found ourselves heading into over-crowded box stores while "nonessential" smaller shops, businesses and yes, houses of worship, were involuntarily shuttered. The logic was hard to figure.

As I have written before to be selective in discrimination is wrong. The state made a mistake, the Governor overreached and now thankfully the Supreme Court has spoken.

HASIDIC WEDDINGS

As I have also written before, the well-publicized albeit "secret" Hasidic wedding with 7,500 attendees was wide off the mark and had no place during this pandemic. Even if you wish to postulate that a Hasidic wedding is a deeply religious experience, which it is, it still has no place when Corona is lurking about and people can, and will, get sick. Who will take the blame if people end up getting sick or making others sick or worse cause them to die? There is nothing religious about this. In fact, the Torah which is where every religion stems from, would tell you that such a wedding is not allowed and the perpetrators should be punished for hurting society. There was nothing holy about attending this wedding and everything unholy. Not wearing masks makes it ten times worse. Not right.

IRRELEVANT TO ME

Regardless of the important Supreme Court decision, I do not plan on taking advantage of it. I could never imagine holding an unsafe event without proper social distancing, masks and continued disinfecting until the all clear is given. I guess you could say I answer to a higher authority. So, while I deeply applaud and appreciate the Justices, for me, it is a moot point.

The way I see it, I am not only accountable to my immediate community, I am also answerable to my greater community, which if you think of it has no real borders or boundaries.

KABBALISTIC INSIGHTS

The "Bible of the Kabbala," the holy book of Zohar was challenged in a Muslim courtroom in Yemen 1914. The anti-kabbalist Jews took the pro-kabbalist Jews to court. The purpose was to forbid Jews from studying Kabbala.

The Muslim ruler of that time, Zaydi ruler of Yemen, Imam Yahya Hamid al-Din, together with the Zaydi Imam found the Zohar acceptable and encouraged its pursuit.

Don't mess with the courts.

TRANSITION OF POWER

A PLEA FOR UNITY

In just over a week, the United States of America will have a new President, Vice President and an entire new administration. From Attorney General to Secretary of Defense, from Secretary of Homeland Security to Secretary of Labor.

PRESIDENTIAL INAUGURATIONS

There have been 72 inaugurations, some private, but mostly public, and not all on the Capitol steps. For the most part the transfer of power from one President to another has been amicable, or at least an attempt at cordiality. Historically, there have been three outgoing Presidents who have refused to attend the inauguration and boycotted it, and it looks like we will see a fourth next week. The first refusal was by President John Adams who was distraught over his loss of the election as well as the death of his son Charles Adams to alcoholism. He left the President's House in the early morning. The next Adams President, son of John Adams, also refused to go to the inauguration of his successor as well as Martin Van Buren for reasons unknown. Obviously, Nixon did not go to Ford's for a different reason and not as a boycott.

JEWISH TRANSFER

The Presidential transfer of power, even with all the recent acrimony, pales in comparison to the Jewish transfer in ancient history. From the first anointed King of Israel, King Saul, until the last day under King Zedekiah, there was nothing but trouble and acrimony, which led to bloodshed, death, captivity and exile.

KING SAUL

Let's take the first King of the United Nation, King Saul. He did not even make it to four years before he was impeached and removed from office. He was deposed by Samuel the Prophet only after two years of rule. He was so crazed at the humility of it all, that he attempted to have the new King by the name of David assassinated before he could be inaugurated. Saul's life ended by suicide in battle so that, this way, he avoided being captured alive by the enemy.

KING DAVID

The next King was David. His life was insane. Aside from being hunted by his predecessor, his own kid Absalom wanted him killed so he could be king. Prior to Absalom's revolt, he made sure to kill his brother Amnon who raped one of their sisters. In the end, Absalom met his demise when his hair got caught in a tree branch and was killed by David's general.

KING SOLOMON

The good news is after all the chaos and treachery, peace finally reigned under King Solomon, at least for a short hiatus, until half the country seceded, and became two kingdoms until it was no more.

WHY THE HISTORY LESSON?

There is a famous quote, "Those who do not remember the past are condemned to repeat it." I firmly believe that we need to look at the history of older civilizations to learn what not to do. The quote that I coined is, "If we do not analyze the past and learn from it, then the future is murky."

THE LESSONS

This is a crucial time for our nation's future. It can go either way.

We can continue to be a fragmented, divided country weakened by all the hate and vitriol, or we can decide to reform and unite for the betterment of our country.

We can politicize everything and have neighbors not talking to each other or we can go back to neighborhood block parties once Covid has been beaten back.

We can fight with our family members and have two Thanksgiving dinners and Passover Seders or we can go back to the way it was where we fight each other at one table.

We can fight completely hidden behind tweets and other social media or we can use social media to help a starving family.

I know what I would choose. How about you?

END GAME

The question that we all need to ask ourselves is what is our end game. What ultimately do we want to see four years from now? A United States or a divided state?

Will our society collapse? Will this great benevolent country turn into a banana republic? We need to be careful and vigilant that it does not.

Sir John Glubb wrote in The Fate of Empires in 1976:

"The life expectation of a great nation, it appears, commences with a violent, and usually unforeseen, outburst of energy, and ends in a lowering of moral standards, cynicism, pessimism and frivolity."

He contrasted 13 different civilizations and found this astonishing fact. Most have only lasted 10 generations or about 250 years.

It is really up to the masses of the United States populace. We need to demand from our politicians, beginning with the three branches of the Federal Government, that they govern with civility, respect and with grace.

If they cannot do this, then maybe it is time for an extreme "home" makeover.

KABBALISTIC INSIGHTS

A leader such as a King, Queen, President or Prime Minister has a special mandate to be proper, just and honorable. We are taught that God made man in his image. If this is true of an average person, then how much more so if it is a person that has influence over thousands or millions. Extra special care must be taken by the leader to be an example and a force for good. Otherwise, it hampers our faith in the ultimate ruler.

ANTI-SEMITISM

ANTI-SEMITIC CONFUSION

STRAIGHT TALK

I recently wrote an article as to how the watered down resolution by Congress in response to the anti-Semitic remarks by a freshman Congresswoman was wrong. I opined that the Congress, as our leader, should have called her out by name and with purpose, instead of pussyfooting around for fear of insulting this one and another. My main point was that unchecked anti-Semitism is a very dangerous game, one that we Jews have played at the losing end for millennia.

There were many responses and comments that generally fit into three categories. The first category I am completely dismissing, since it was from anti-Semitic trolls on social media with catch phrases like "from the river to the sea, Palestine will be free," which is essentially a slogan used to make a point that Israel's Jews will be thrown and drowned into the sea and Israel will be Judenrein.

I am dismissing them not because it does not bother me that there are people who hate me and my people. I am dismissing them because my article and thoughts had nothing to do with Israel, and only to do with anti-Semitic tropes and the poor ensuing response. There are times when being anti-Israel can be anti-Semitic and organizations like the BDS and SJP are guilty time and time again on conflating the two, conveniently I might add. Linda Sarsour, as an example, runs on a BDS platform and we all know who she really is. So, category 1 – dismissed easily. Just not worth my time.

The second category of people who replied were either those who agreed or wanted to know more about what was said. Once educated as to the Congresswoman's quotes on how Israel hypnotizes the world, follows the Benjamins and that US Jews have dual loyalties and allegiances to a foreign power, they were satisfied that we are dealing with a person who should have been censured harshly. One of our Jewish holidays is *Purim* where Jews all over are celebrated with great enthusiasm. If you pay any attention to the story, it was an Omar moment. The wicked Haman accused the Jews of being disloyal to the crown, and therefore, worthy of being annihilated.

To everyone's astonishment Congress decided to resolve that all mean comments are inappropriate, including hate against Latinos, Asian Americans, Muslims, Hindus, Sikhs, Pacific Islanders, Native Americans, immigrants and the LGBTQ community, and oh yes, Jews as well. I have no idea as to what the objection was to setting her straight, especially as she is a repeat offender. I do believe that every member of Congress should be held to the highest standards and this is part and parcel of government. As stated earlier, these types of comments are highly inflammatory and must be kept in check.

The last category of responders is definitely the most troubling to me. Their knee-jerk reaction to my knee-jerk reaction to anti-Semitism is immediately placed into the realm of politics. They lambast me because I want a censure of a "Democrat." Or, they write things like Steven King or President Trump are the real racists here. Why bring party politics into this? This is simply a right or wrong issue and not a left or right one.

Let me set the record straight. Aside from these being stupid comments, they are also dangerous as they detract from what was said and create a smoke-screen that obfuscates the problem at hand. My standard is this. If you spew anti-Semitic garbage then you are a bad egg. Period. End of sentence. A politician's platform, however noble, is meaningless to me if you are a Jew-hater or any type of hater for that matter.

A few principles that I live by:

1. All good people need to call out anti-Semitism, no matter where it comes from, regardless of political party. Steven King and Ilhan Omar are both guilty as charged. I do not believe in giving any of them a pass due to political convictions.

2. To remain silent in the face of anti-Semitism is abhorrent, since every pogrom we have suffered in our long history has been due to the silence of people when the "spaghetti began to hit the fan."

3. I am unable to respect any person who places their political party over principles and morals. In other words, I cannot even reach a place where I agree to disagree because when it comes to anti-Semitism, with comments like dual loyalties, there is no wiggle room for me over this. I feel that my kid's and your kid's lives are at stake.

4. I agree with Senator Joseph Lieberman that no party is anti-Semitic in this country, but rather, there are individuals in Congress who are. I maintain that they need to be censured. Why should this be so hard?

KABBALISTIC INSIGHTS

Maimonides in his Guide to the Perplexed posits that there are three types of evil in this world.

The first is evil caused by nature.

The second is evil what people bring upon others.

The third is what an evil man brings upon himself.

Maimonides fleshes them all out. In his explanation of the second evil, which humans bring upon others, he states that is an extremely rare evil. He proves this by writing, "If we are to look at the world in its entirety, there is more good than bad."

I live by this principle. Sure, there are rotten people out there. In my opinion, they are the vocal minority.

DON'T JUST STAND AGAINST ANTI-SEMITISM

DO SOMETHING ABOUT IT

Ever so often on Facebook, there is a slogan that is created to reflect the current mood of many people. One example was when there was a shooting at a kosher French shop in Paris and many people posted on their wall the words "Je suis Juif." This literally means "I am a Jew," or non-literally, "I stand with the Jews and I am appalled that Jews were targeted."

After the latest craze of anti-Semitic incidents in New York where Jews all over the city were being beaten to the ground, many different and worthy organizations came up with slogans like, "I stand against anti-Semitism." Well, I don't! I do not want to be known as someone who stands against anti-Semitism, rather, I want to DO something about it. I want to be in front of it and not behind it. I want to be proactive and not just offer a feel-good pump fist in the air. I wish to inspire all who read this to be action oriented as well.

So, practically speaking, what can we do in 2020 to stop or at least slow the disease, scourge, menace and plague of Jew-hating bigots and thugs?

MORAL ROT

I, like you, have been watching videos of the aforementioned attacks, and they all have one thing in common. What I witnessed in horror was that the greater public on the streets of New York did nothing to protect the victim. I saw a Yeshiva student being harassed, garbage thrown at him and tormented, and yet not one person on the street came to his rescue. The cars continued to drive by or park, the pedestrians crossed the street to avoid confrontation and the store owners continued to hawk their wares. This is unacceptable and is called MORAL ROT. When good people do nothing then this is a tacit approval that all is okay in la la land.

Put down the latte and start calling others on the street to help this poor victim. When the holy Torah commands us in Leviticus Chapter 19, "Do not stand idly by while your neighbor's blood is shed," it does not only mean marching for gun control or ending animal abuse. IT MEANS LITERALLY–STOP THE BLOODSHED. In the words of the great Rabbi Abraham Joshua Heschel, "In a free society, only some may be guilty but all are responsible."

Cowardice, weakness, timidity, and fearfulness are all words to describe spinelessness. Be inspired to stop the moral rot.

REPEAL CATCH & RELEASE

The new laws to hit the New York state are a danger to all the good citizens and are a haven and shelter for thugs. The new law basically states that bail is a thing of the past unless the perp draws blood. It is madness! You can fire a gun in the air, hit someone, rob at gun point or spit at a Jew, and as long as you do not draw blood, you will be released at your own recognizance and right back on the street.

A recent true story, a woman assaulted three Jewish women, got arrested, was released and then promptly, that very day, assaulted someone again, and was released AGAIN. This same Tiffany Harris according to the New York Post, has a record of assault in 2018, and she has not shown up for other court dates in the past. She is a scofflaw and a threat to human beings. She is being treated better than we are. She needs to cool her jets in a prison. Don't be a sideliner. Call your state assemblyman and state senator. Call the Governor and get people like her off the street. I did. My assemblyman is in agreement that the new law is insanity at best, and kowtowing for votes at its worst.

I understand the reason behind the law. I agree that there should be catch and release, but never for a violent person. It is not fair, and when something is not fair, then we the people should not be silent.

Read the following and be inspired.

"Each time a man or woman stands up for an ideal, or acts to improve the lot of others, they send forth a tiny ripple of hope, and crossing each other from a million different centers of energy and daring, those tiny ripples can build a current that can sweep down the mightiest walls of oppression and resistance." – Robert Kennedy.

BE PROUD

As a Rabbi, I am stopped by a great many Jewish people in the street, in the supermarket and even in the DMV. They tell me that they are scared. They tell me that this year they are not placing their Chanukah menorah in the window for fear of anti-Semitic thugs.

My response is always the same. Do not let thugs, hooligans and hate-filled people dictate what you do or do not do.

You are a Jew – be proud!

If you hide your Jewishness out of fear or discomfort, then they have won the battle. We must not let them be victorious. Ironically, the very story of Chanukah depicts this message. The Jews refused to let the Greeks dictate what is okay to do and believe. They fought back. We need to add in our Jewish pride at this time and God forbid, not retreat.

God Bless. May the stank of anti-Semites be washed away by good people standing up for our people.

KABBALISTIC INSIGHTS

The squeaky wheel gets oiled is a famous proverb. What it means is that someone who complains or is more vocal will receive the attention.

The Torah tells us the story of the five daughters of Tzelafchad who died and left no sons, only daughters. Initially, Moses was told by God to divide the land of Israel via head of household. Since Tzelafchad passed there was no head of household, and these young women were overlooked.

That was until they became very vocal and questioned the fairness of it all. Moses conversed with God, and indeed it was determined that they will receive a land allotment.

We need to be vocal. Silence is acquiescence.

KABBALAH OF THE INNER ANTI-SEMITE

HOW TO CONFRONT THE ENEMY WITHIN

As we are approaching the Jewish holiday of *Purim*, which celebrates the downfall of the arch anti-Semite Haman, I would like to discuss a novel concept called the hidden enemy. While there have been plenty of anti-Semites over the years who have been beaten back, Haman's downfall is Jewishly – universally celebrated because of a couple of factors.

1. HIGH RANKING CABINET MEMBER

One important factor was that he was not simply a thug on the street, but rather he occupied a very lofty position in an equally powerful government. Imagine a vice-president spewing anti-Semitic diatribe and rousing the populace to beat, torture and punish Jews because they are Jews.

2. FAMILY CONNECTIONS.

The second reason, and this will be the focus of my short thoughts, is that Haman was not a first generation anti-Semite, but rather he comes from a long line of delusional, drunk and insane anti-Semites. This Haman creep had Jew hatred coursing through his veins. He was indoctrinated while sitting on his great grandpa's lap as to how bad the Jews are.

Who was his "illustrious" family?

The Purim Megillah/scroll calls him Haman the Aggagite, meaning he stems from Agag. Who was Agag? Agag, we are taught in the Scriptures, was the king of a ferocious tribe called Amalek. Agag was a ruthless king who constantly waged war with the ancient Israelites in the times of King Saul. What is interesting is that Agag himself was inculcated with vile and rabid Jew hatred while he too was sitting on his great grandpa King Amalek's lap.

QUESTION

Who are the Amalekites and what is their beef with Jews?

CLASSIC ANSWER

As recorded in the Torah/Bible, the Amalekites were the first nation to attack the Jews upon their Exodus. While all the nations heard the great miracles that occurred to the Jews, when they saw the havoc that was brought upon Pharaoh and the Egyptians, the surrounding nations stood in awe with jaws open and trembling knees. All but one that is. The Amalekites immediately attacked the Hebrews from behind and killed off the slower folk. By doing this, they broke the "Jewish" spell that the nations were under. A war ensued, the Hebrews beat the Amalekites, and they became the sworn enemy.

KABBALISTIC VIEW

According to the more esoteric approach, the issue with the Amalekites is not that they broke the spell that the surrounding nations were under, but rather, they broke the magical feelings and exuberance that the Hebrews were feeling. The Hebrews went from immense faith after witnessing incredible miracles and wonders in Egypt and at the Sea of Reeds, to feeling bewildered that they were attacked and people were killed. They went from being passionately and madly in love with God to feeling let down by God. The Kabbalah teaches us that what Amalekites did was to instill doubt and confusion in the hearts of the Hebrews, which ultimately led to apathy and indifference. They played with our emotions and toyed with our faith. The Kabbalah goes on to explain that it is for this reason that Amalek is our arch enemy, because Amalek represents an uninspiring and fed-up human. Someone who is uninspired and worn out and is spiritually bankrupt, is a sad existence.

So, when the wicked Haman who represents Amalek who represents dullness of the heart is beaten, then it is time to celebrate because when we can close the chapter of spiritual bankruptcy, then it is truly a time to celebrate.

In conclusion, the Kabbalah imparts the following incredible thought. It is much better to be passionate about an issue even if it is antithetical to God, than to be dull and apathetic. You see, passion can be redirected and rearranged, but apathy is very difficult to change and redirect. Apathy, teaches the Kabbalah, is the enemy within, which if allowed to continue can rot someone's emotions from the inside. It may begin with a benign "not in the mood" type of feeling and end up causing someone to decay spiritually. While Amalek is a physical anti-Semite, tedium, weariness and dreariness is its spiritual counterpart.

Be passionate. Be ardent. Be zealous. As long as you got the fire burning.

KABBALISTIC INSIGHTS

The Zohar relates the Hebrew word for "in happiness." (b'simcha) contains exactly the same letters as the Hebrew word for "thought" (machshava).

What this means is that it is up to us through the gift given by God, that our minds are able to control and weed out negative emotions.

OUTRAGE ON CAMPUS

THE POWER IS IN OUR HANDS

It never ceases to amaze me. We live in the United States of America, in the land of the free and the home of the brave in the year 2020 and yet, we Jews and moral people are being literally maligned on a daily basis on campuses across the USA. And there is nothing being done to stop this madness.

Every day there are horror stories about Jews being verbally assaulted or a university bringing out dangerous and hateful speakers. Or the university allowing a pro-Palestinian conference to be held on its grounds for its students and faculty, which creates such distortions of truth and accomplishes one thing and one thing only - anti-Semitism. The university usually cowers under the "free speech" clause, as slowly lives become intolerable.

The worst part of this horrific story is that there are still wealthy Jews, in the spirit of philanthropy, continuing to dish out money to these "houses of higher hate." Don't get me wrong, I am not telling these families where to put their money; I am saying that I don't understand how some of these families are silent in the face of NYU and UMass Amherst anti-Israel and anti-Jewish conferences that are taking place.

The ridicule that Jewish college students have to go through on a daily basis on some college campuses is not unlike what Jews in Berlin had to go through in the late 1920's and early 1930's. Where is the Jewish pride? Where is the warning from these philanthropists, as an example, to the Chancellor Kumble R. Subbaswamy of UMass who has allowed rabid dogs like Roger "polluted" Waters and Linda "opportunist" Sarsour to speak at the campus more than once? Why is this allowed to continue?

There was recently an anti-Semitic, pro-Palestinian two-day conference that took place at the University of Michigan – Ann Arbor. Students for Justice in Palestine (SJP) held their national Midwest conference. EVERY group registered at this conference had ties to terror. In fact, Visa, MC and PayPal all refuse to deal with any of them. So, if the financial payment giants say no to terror, why isn't the University of Michigan? Where is the outrage? Why is the Board, consisting of people like Mark Schlissel, Michael J. Behm, and Mark Bernstein, silent while this is going on?

My friends, the inmates are running the asylum and I am sad to tell you that help is not coming unless you and I get involved. This will not be stopped organically by any Board of Trustees or wealthy donors, this will only be stopped when we get together and become vocal opponents of this madness. I cannot explain fully as to why this craziness, detestation and hatred is not stopped by the people in power. I can only assume that it is because of political correctness gone awry. Regardless, it will not get better unless we implement some of the following.

Practically speaking:

1. We need to stop sending our kids into the fires of hell. We need to gather around campuses that stand up to this daily garbage and put their foot down. If you are a campus that allows SJP in your sacred halls, then we say go to hell. We will not send our kids while you weak, pathetic and cowardly morons allow groups associated with terrorists to parade down your hallways. Your degrees mean nothing if you are impotent to stop this. Shame on you.

2. We need to begin legal action. There is a federal law that protects students called the Title VI of the Civil Rights Act of 1964. You may file a discrimination complaint either in court or with the Office for Civil Rights in the US Department of Education. Enough complaints and who knows maybe this will stop.

3. Appeal to donors of these colleges and universities to have a conversation with the Board to stop it. Michigan has huge donors like Sam Zell (szell@egii.com), Ron Weiser and Stephen Ross. They need to be reached as well as the Tisch family. They need letters and emails sent to their homes and businesses imploring them to have the conversation.

This can be stopped. Sarsour can be stopped. BDS can be stopped. SJP can be stopped.

We need to be proactive and assertive. It is up to us. This is no time to be apathetic or to be a voyeur.

KABBALSITIC INSIGHTS

This is perhaps your moment. There is a wonderful teaching that puts it in perspective. This is from a holy book called Hayom Yom.

The Alter Rebbe received the following teaching from the tzadik Reb Mordechai, who had heard it from the Baal Shem Tov: A soul may descend to this world and live seventy or eighty years, in order to do a material favor, and certainly a spiritual one.

YOU need to act.

JEWISH ANTI SEMITES?

A LETTER TO SETH ROGEN

In the beginning of his interview with Marc Maron, he mentioned, "If you are an anti-Semite, you will be triggered." Well, after listening to your interview Seth, I disagree completely. I believe that any anti-Semite that listened to you rant about Israel was thrilled. I know I was triggered. Every Jew I know was triggered. However, the anti-Semites are coming out in droves praising you. If you go on Twitter as an example, you will see all the known and not known anti-Semites, as well as self-haters applaud you. Personally, Seth, I would rather die than have Linda Sarsour praise me for my words.

MY GOAL WITH THIS LETTER

While the damage you caused with your quips on Israel is nothing short of horrific and you should be ashamed of yourself, I do not want to focus on your dishonor, but rather on the Jewish pride. I want to educate your admirers (not one anymore) on the truth about Israel because clearly you are ignorant and absolutely clueless. Hopefully, your followers will realize that Jewish history is not your strong suit, and while you may know a thing or two about making pickles, you know very little of what we have lived through.

THANKS TO ISRAEL

I know you said that Israel does not make sense. A quick thought as to why it is imperative that Israel exists. Modern day Israel was founded as a refuge to millions of Jews who were at risk of ethnic cleansing. Far fewer Jews have died in Israel than they have in the diaspora over equal number of years, throughout history. And there is a government that protects them. Would you rather it does not exist Seth, and have history repeat itself? I believe at last count we lost six million Jews. I know anti-Semites have been pretty upset that Israel has saved potentially millions of lives. I still do not get what your beef is.

THE OCCUPIER MYTH

How terrible, you shared with millions, that you were "fed a huge amount of lies about Israel my entire life! They never tell you that – oh by the way, there were people there. They make it seem like it was just like sitting there, like the (obscenity) door's open they forget to include the fact to every young Jewish person."

Boy did you put your foot instead of a pickle in your mouth. A huge chunk of shoe leather. Seth, maybe you really should study a little more about the history of your people.

Yes, there were other people in Palestine. But even a hostile world somehow recognized, first by way of the San Remo solution (Google it Seth) and then with United Nations recognition (Google it Seth), that amidst a sea of newly created Arab countries, Jews had a right to at least a tiny sliver of land they could call their own, again after a lengthy hiatus.

Seth, Jews had nowhere to go. I know you have no clue that in 1948 the Arab world (Sarsour & Tlaib's world) expelled about 850,000 Jews from their lands. Jews had lived in the Arab lands for thousands of years, and many of their communities preceded the advent of Islam. But in the 20th century, with the rise of Arab nationalism and the conflict in Palestine, the new Arab regimes began a campaign of massive violations of rights of their Jewish citizens. Arab states stole property of their native Jews, and denaturalized, expelled, arrested, tortured and murdered many of them.

The Arab countries, which never accepted the UN declaration on the establishment of a Jewish state, compelled the Jews living in their territories to leave their homes while leaving all their assets behind. In several instances, the deportations were accompanied by pogroms and violence against Jews.

Let's take Iraq for example, the Jewish community of Iraq had existed for more than 2,500 years and was a cultural center of Judaism where the Babylonian Talmud was written and compiled. This ancient community came under attack from the Iraqi government in the wake of the establishment of Israel, and was expelled, after being physically attacked with many fatalities, and their property and assets confiscated.

You see Seth, you and the Arab world cannot have it both ways. You cannot complain that Israel took over land but not take responsibility of what they did to the Jews in addition to the Nazis, of which many collaborated. Can you imagine Seth, your family living in Vancouver, and then being kicked out after establishing roots there simply because you were the wrong ("silly in your words") religion?

CLARITY AND FACTS

Dig a little more Seth and you will discover and unearth these two astonishing facts:

1. There was no Palestinian state in 1967 or any time before that.

2. Israel did not occupy East Jerusalem, The West Bank and Gaza any time between 1948 and 1967! READ THAT AGAIN. Israel did NOT occupy Jerusalem and the other territories. Wow.

You will then ask yourself and wonder why Abbas and Arafat did not declare a Palestinian state during the 19 years between 1948 and 1967. They had close to 19 years to declare a state but failed to do so. You then think into this a little more and you have to conclude that it is strange. You see, Israel declared a state in May of 1948 on the VERY same date that the British Mandate expired. So, one state gets declared within a few hours and the other state cannot get its act together over the course of 19 years! You must conclude that something is fishy here.

You see Seth, the Israelis wanted their part of a two-state solution, but the Palestinians did not. Did you not learn this Seth?

What is amazing is that Abbas, Arafat and the other "leaders" refuse to speak about the times between 1948 and 1967. It is as if they do not exist. Abbas chooses rather to grandstand at the UN rather than be an honest and peaceful leader and end the self-afflicted refugee crisis that these leaders created in the first place.

APOLOGY

Seth, awaiting your proper apology without your mother having to beg you to do so. Your people need you to undo what you have done. Do it soon while the haters are still rubbing their hands together in glee.

KABBALISTIC INSIGHTS

The origin of Jews disparaging other Jews has been going on for millennia. It is only recently that it seems to reflect the disagreements over Israel

The Talmud records the feud between various factions and sects of Jews, that eventually lead to the destruction of the second temple. Infighting, shaming, disparaging and arguing between ourselves is so deleterious, that it was the sole cause that sent the Jews into exile which has lasted two thousand years.

THE 7 HABITS OF AN ANTI-SEMITE

AN EXPOSÉ ON ANTI-SEMITISM

One of the hottest topics to hit social media and news outlets of late is the one surrounding anti-Semitism. Even news outlets that generally do not hold Jews in a good light are shining a weak spotlight on the plight of Jews being verbally harassed or physically abused by Jew haters coming from all sides of the political spectrum. From Pittsburgh to Poway, New Jersey to New York, there has been a record amount of attacks.

Everyone is pointing fingers at everyone. The right to the left and the left to the right. Regardless, I do not wish to turn this into another political circus. Truth be told, anti-Semitism is a tale as old as time and it definitely precedes Washington DC, the South side of Chicago or Louisiana. The question is why?

My kid asked me this exact question the other day in the form of the following question, "What did we Jews do so bad for people to hate us enough to kill us in grocery stores and synagogues?" While I do not think the answer is that complex, I do believe that there are many facets to why Jew-hatred exists.

The first thing I tell anyone when asked this question is that most people are good, decent, moral and upstanding and simply want to live and let live. So, while anti-Semitism is high, it is a vocal minority.

You know the book by Stephen Covey titled *The 7 types of Highly Effective People?* Here I present the 7 types of rotten anti-Semites. Unlike Covey's book, this will not be a bestseller. I do believe though, that it should be a classic.

Why you ask am I doing this? I believe in the adage that knowing the sickness is half the cure. There are some anti-Semites who are curable and some who are not. It is Important to discern.

DISEASE OF THE MIND

Yes, part of anti-Semitism is that there is something wrong with the person. The efforts and resources such as money spent on ways to hurt Jews are a clear indicator that they are sick and have a mental disorder. Falling into this category would be someone like Roger Waters. He is an incurable sick individual. He has all the fame, love, money and importance, yet he chooses to hurl and spew his diatribe instead of focusing on more positive things. Even his ex-wife would agree that he is sick. He is seen in a video in his bathrobe, high as a kite spewing his verbal diarrhea. The only conundrum I have with someone like this is, do I pray for health to be restored or a quick/slow demise? By the way, this is where I would also classify Mel Gibson. Once again, has it all – just very sick and a nasty drunk to boot.

EVIL

For whatever reason, God chose to populate our world with bad people. Some of them really bad, also known as evil. They are sadistic and take great pleasure in causing pain. Most of them are also cowards. Take Hitler and Saddam Hussein as examples. They hid in their respective bunkers like rats, and Hitler, the leader of the 1000 Year (really 7 years, but let's not be petty) Reich blew his brains out so that he would not be caught and held responsible. Pol Pot, Joseph Stalin, Ivan Grozny – they are all examples of wicked people in the flesh who enjoyed killing, maiming and assaulting fellow human beings. Because Jews stick out as a moral compass, the need to get rid of them is akin to needing a drink after being in a desert for three days. Louis Farrakhan would probably fit into this category and/or the next one.

RACE BAITING OPPORTUNISTS

It has been proven over the years that a "great" cause produces much money. Louis Farrakhan's Nation of Islam is worth over $75 million. Not bad for hot air. Al Sharpton just gave himself a $450,000 raise on top of his $250,000 salary. National Action Network raises millions per annum. If all were quiet then the money flow would slow to a halt.

The Romans needed money so they beat nations into submission with hangings and swords. No different – just a little more sophisticated.

Therefore, the race baiters need to assure that all is not quiet and this is why Farrakhan and Sarsour are so active. Why the Jews? Easy bait and quick money.

IGNORANCE/FEAR OF THE OTHER

There is not much good to be said about this category either. This group hates, despises and is disgusted because you do not fit into a certain mold. Rather than take the time to be human and learn something new in this world, they resort to hate and revulsion. They hate all people equally. They hate Jews, blacks, Latinos, etc. They have not and will not evolve. Money is secondary to them. Hate is the primary reason for living. KKK and militia groups are what we are dealing with here. Some of them are slick like Richard Spencer in a nice suit and tie or David Duke, but most are not.

JEALOUSY

Plain old and simple jealousy. When they see successful Jews in real estate, Hollywood or finance, the anti-Semites see red. There is no credit given for the fact that the successful Jew (or anyone) worked their body to the bone to get to this coveted position. Hundreds of hours per week at work, sacrificing basics such as family time, vacations, extended family reunions and on and on.

Add to this, the length of time spent in college while the anti-Semite watched reruns of Family Guy and Smokey and the Bandit. This college student agonized over the MCAT or the LSAT or whatever graduate school entry test they needed to do to be considered for a graduate school. Jews are a people of the book so we study.

The jealous boor sees nothing other than jealousy. The jealous churl simply wants to know why this guy drives a BMW and he drives a used Chevy Spark. Over time, the jealousy festers and eventually rears its ugly head and justifies its boorish behavior.

HISTORICAL

Now we get to the historical anti-Semite. The ones that believe if they stop hating the Jew, then all previous decades that their ancestors fought will be for naught. Furthermore, the hate has been so ingrained that they cannot do anything about it.

Luckily, there are many who move geographically away from the hate and become deprogrammed. Unfortunately, there are many like the Tlaibs and Omars (2019 anti-Semite of the year – Mazal Tov) of the world. It is in their blood and there is nothing anyone can say or do about it. It is so sad to be steeped in hate that it oozes from their pores. Do not be fooled, this has nothing to do with Israel and 1948. Tlaib's ancestors happily hacked off Jewish body parts in the Hebron massacre of 1929.

Truth be told, inculcating one's child to hate so ferociously is a form of child abuse. Handing out candies when a Jew is killed is child abuse. Having one's child see you dance when the twin towers came down is child abuse.

THE GOONIES

Our final dog would be the goons, the followers, lackeys, minions, underlings, gofers and zombies who just follow the pack. There is no ideology involved other than just copy what they see others do. This final category has no thought or creed or excuse.

If you are an anti-Semite reading this or you know an anti-Semite and for the life of you cannot figure out what drives them, then this is probably it.

Now we have gotten my thoughts on the whys, we need to zero in to see what we can do about it.

Can we help them?

Can we get them to see the light?

Is it curable?

What to do?

More forthcoming.

KABBALISTIC INSIGHTS

To be a leader is not only a gift from God, it comes with tremendous responsibility. Essentially, a leader is chosen for whatever reason to guide, shepherd, direct and inspire others.

When a leader abuses this gift, and instead of inspiring people to be their better selves, and helping others, the leader causes rift, destruction and brings out the worst in people, it is a mortal sin.

The Talmud has some "nice" things to say about a sinner that causes many others to sin.

7 WAYS TO COMBAT ANTI-SEMITISM

TRIED & PROVEN

We have previously discussed the seven types of anti-Semites and why they exist. To recap briefly - 1. The Nutjob 2. Jealousy 3. Evil People 4. Race Baiter Opportunists 5. Ignorant and Fearful 6. Historical 7. The Goonies/Followers/The Weak.

Each of the above categories feels justified to hate the Jew. For some of them the hatred is so rabid and visceral, that it actually effects their life and wellbeing. Their problem — not mine. What is my problem is what I do about it, or more likely, what we do about the hate.

I have come up with seven responses to hate which, in actuality, will not make them hate us any less, but will allow us to survive as a people and to be the first responder in combatting anti-Semitism. You see, as Jews we are not unlike canaries in the coalmine who can detect trouble before the miners. The savages may come for us first, but by all means, they will not stop with only the Jews. Case in point, when the world looked on at the intifada, which included suicide attacks happening in Israel, and clicked their respective tongues and shook their respective heads but did nothing to help, the savages upped the game and they started to attack, kill, maim and beat other nationalities in other parts of the world. So, take heed, our response to anti-Semitism is not only for Jews but for mankind as well.

FIGHT BACK

Pick up a shovel and fight back. Simple as that. Anti-Semites are a cowardly bunch and have no tolerance for difficult hate. They prefer to be 3 on 1 and not 1 on 1. I am not advocating anarchy; I am simply stating be active and not only reactive. Better safe than sorry. If you see something then DO something. The time for Chamberlain passivity has long passed. (Not sure there ever was a time). We need to be prepared to stand up to be stronger, better and more courageous than they are.

ECONOMIC BOYCOTT

Taking a line straight out of their playbook. Do not purchase any item whatsoever from an anti-Semitic owned business. Not one more Roger Waters upload and no donating to Ilhan Omar's PAC or to Jewish Voice for Peace (JVP). This is a very effective way of sending a message.

CHOOSING THE RIGHT CAMPUS

Continuing the above theme … We as parents spend way too much money to send our kids to school as it is. So, therefore, if a college campus has either anti-Semitic faculty with undue influence or a campus that has literally uncontrolled hate and bigotry in it with no limits, then rest assured that the dean's office and its Board have given, at the very least, a tacit nod. Colleges like UMass Amherst, who has invited Linda Sarsour not once but twice, should not be given any respect, even the $75 application fee. Please realize that the college campus is the frontlines of where this anti-Semitic war is being held. Choose carefully how bloody you want that war to be.

BE UNIFIED

Squabbling amongst ourselves is probably the worst thing we can do, especially publicly. This will cause the hater to implement a divide and conquer strategy in order to weaken us. We need to stand together as a united front. As an example, when Jews pay homage to the fanatical leader of Iran by either flying to see him or expressing love on Facebook, then this hurts all of us. We need to stay strong together as one family unit. We need to remember that when they hurt one of us then they hurt us all. I shake my head in disbelief at the levels of acrimony that exists between Jews. If Hitler taught us anything, it is that he never cared what type of Jew you were.

SUPPORT ISRAEL

Regardless of your opinion on Israel, supporting Israel is a must and the only moral thing to do. The difference between Germany 1933 and France 2020 is Israel. Israel is the ace up our sleeve. It is the one advantage that our poor grandparents never had in Eastern Europe. It is the key, the answer if you will, to our very survival. So, don't be quick to knock it, boycott it or tread on it, as you may need it yourself one day, especially considering the current political climate.

BUILD SECURELY

There is no question that we as Jews need to continue building hospitals, nursing homes, synagogues, businesses, schools, Yeshivas and Jewish Community Centers. We need to be powerful and strong and we need to continue to do the good that we do. So, the first message is continue expanding and not be afraid. There is a caveat though — build securely. Spend some of the building money on safety and security. Be vigilant and be safe.

BE PROUD

Don't even think of shirking the kippah because of anti-Semitism. On the contrary, instead of scaling anything back, we need to enhance our Jewishness and Jewish awareness. We need to show the savages that we are proud of who we are and we are unashamed and unabashed. We are the people who brought morals and values to the world. If they choose to buck these morals and be morons, then this is their choice. We are messengers for a good world. Shooting the messengers will not stop the message from being carried out.

KABBALISTIC INSIGHTS

I left the most important one, last. Throughout our long and sordid history, Jews have resorted to prayer. The story of Purim comes to mind. There was a terrible decree on the Jewish people in ancient Persia and beyond.

The heroes of the story, both Esther and Mordechai strategized using many of the tools listed above. The first thing they did however, was to gather as many Jews as they could to join together in prayer.

This strategy we learned from our Patriarchs and Matriarchs thousands of years ago.

THE THREE JACKSONS

FARRAKHAN AND DIVISION

Those of you who are familiar with my observations and me know that I have a very clear opinion of what is right and wrong. I am not a grey type of person. I call it as I see it. I am human so I can be wrong as only God is error free. I do have a couple of fundamental beliefs when it comes to anti-Semitism. The first being that we need to be is vocal and never silent as silence is acquiescence. The second is that anyone who supports an anti-Semite is immoral, even if they are not per se, anti-Semitic.

Let's examine a few recent outspoken anti-Semites and try to get a handle on what makes them tick. I do believe that most honorable people would find the following disturbing.

JACKSON #1

NFL player and Philadelphia Eagles wide-receiver DeSean Jackson shared a series of Instagram posts that included a quote with terrible anti-Jewish language (*refuse to write it here*). Jackson's original post follows a July 4th weekend where he spent a considerable amount of time watching and listening to Minister Louis Farrakhan, the controversial leader of the Nation of Islam, with Jackson posting several times about his hours-long speech in the days since. "This man powerful," Jackson said. "I hope everyone got a chance to watch this!! Don't be blinded. Know what's going on!!"

Jackson has since apologized multiple times, and in a lengthy statement addressed the core criticisms of his posts.

"I post a lot of things that are sent to me. I do not have hatred towards anyone. I really didn't realize what this passage was saying. Hitler has caused terrible pain to Jewish people like the pain African-Americans have suffered," Jackson wrote. "This was a mistake to post this and I truly apologize for posting it and sorry for any hurt I have caused."

JACKSON #2

Ex-NBA star Stephen Jackson also praised Farrakhan in defense of the first Jackson during an Instagram Live session, while also expressing love for the Jewish people.

He said, "I'm a fan of Minister Farrakhan because nobody loves Black people more than him and that's just facts. I'm my own man. I believe what I want to believe and I love everybody else. But I love the Minister. … He's teaching me how to be a leader. I'm my own person. I do what I wanna do. I know how to love the Minister and love Jewish people too." Well, he may say he loves the Jewish people, but he also commented the following on Instagram, "You know who the Rothschilds are? They own all the banks."

Hmmmm. Seems very Farrakhani to me.

Listen dude. It is impossible to love Louis F. and the Jews. It is a contradiction. You have to take your pick. Let's put this another way. Who are you going to side with when the two "loves" conflict?

JACKSON # 3

A few days after Jackson # 2 spoke out, Jackson # 3 reared his head. As reported by the media, Eagles defensive linemen Malik Jackson referred to Farrakhan as "honorable" in a since-deleted tweet that read as follows, "the honorable Farrakhan is nothing like that vile scum Hitler." He went on to downplay the anti-Semitic message DeSean posted as he (Jackson #1) did not quote anyone, he just took a picture of a book.

ANALYSIS

There are two common denominators with the Jackson 3.

1. They are beyond ignorant as to the hell Jews have been through. They just parrot what they hear without looking for themselves. It is only when they got caught in a firestorm, did they backtrack. If the NFL did not raise an eyebrow, Jackson #1 would have not backstepped and Jackson 2 and 3 would still be in Farrakhan bliss.

2. The Jackson 3 are still okay with Farrakhan being a racist bigot, which is deplorable. Farrakhan has never hidden what he thinks of the Jews. He has been racist-baiting a long time. In fact, the United Kingdom has banned him for his racism since 1986. Unfortunately, in the U.S. he has visits, handshakes and hugs from those that sit in the high seats of Government. Shameful.

3. Technically there are 4 Jacksons as in Jesse Jackson. Leave him for now.

FARRAKHAN THROUGHOUT THE AGES

Louis X, as he is called, is a proud Holocaust Denier. In a 2014 speech he railed that "the satanic Jews that control everything, and mostly everybody, if they are your enemy, you must, must be somebody." In an October 2018 speech, Farrakhan referred to Jews as termites: "So when they talk about Farrakhan, call me a hater, you know what they do, call me an anti-Semite. Stop it, I'm anti-Termite."

And on and on and on.

In conclusion, it enrages me to hear people quote him, meet him, shake his hand, take his picture and defend him. As I said above, anyone who supports an anti-Semite is immoral.

KABBALISTIC INSIGHTS

It would have been great if God did not create evil. One of the reasons given as to why he did create evil, is to help us maintain our free will.

God gave us the power to sift through lies amidst truth or truth amidst lies, and hopefully separate good from bad. This is not easy and takes much effort.

RELATIONSHIPS

3 WAYS TO IMPROVE ANY RELATIONSHIP

AN EASY FIX FOR MOST

Over the Jewish holiday of Shavuot, which commemorates the giving of the Torah on Mount Sinai, I heard a lecture given by a brilliant and astute woman by the name of Miriam Yerushalmi. As I always like to learn new things, I took to heart what she said and would like to share her words of wisdom. This is all based on memory as there was no recording.

She basically posited that there are 3 conditions to make any relationship work - whether in a marriage, parenting or even business relationships. The following is a synopsis of her talk with my own commentary in the mix.

SELF LOVE

There is a well known Biblical verse, which states, "Love your neighbor as yourself." Seemingly this is impossible. How do you love someone as yourself? Everyone knows that self-love is much stronger than love of neighbor. Think about it. If there is one bag of salt left in Home Depot and it is incredibly icy on your driveway, do you give the bag to your neighbor or do you de-ice your own dangerous driveway? Of course, you make sure that you and your family are safe first and foremost, and this is in fact the right thing to do. So, what does this verse mean?

We all know that self-love is blind. In other words, we know that we have glaring personality flaws that have been with us for a long time and chances are, not going away any time soon. And yet, we seem to function quite well despite the knowledge that we are positively flawed. This concept of overlooking flaws is true with regards to others. The verse states. Love them as you love yourself. They may have glaring flaws and issues, but instead of pointing them out, gloss over them as you do to your own faults. Move on and don't get caught up in someone's issues.

BE QUIET

When someone is talking to you to try and get their point across you need to be quiet. Did you know that the word listen and the word silent are made up of the same letters? This is a critical ingredient. If you attempt to answer back when a person is talking to you, then you are not listening but are rather thinking about your response.

Hear them out, listen to what they have to say and only then think and respond. This way the person will have felt heard at the very least even if they are not agreed with.

COMPASSION

The last and probably the most important part to this, is compassion.

We simply never know what is transpiring in someone else's life. Even if the person is smiling from ear to ear it is no proof that everything is hunky dory. Likewise, if your spouse, child or partner acts out of character then it could be because of something that they are going through that perhaps you do not know nothing about.

The Kabballah teaches that there are three ways to tackle a spouse, child or any other relationship. The first is with unrestrained kindness. The problem with unbridled kindness is sometimes it can teach a bad lesson as the person may not deserve what it is you are giving them. Discipline can work but only in rare instances, but otherwise discipline mostly backfires unless it is tempered with kindness.

Compassion however, says the Kabballah is a perfect blend of love and discipline and therefore should be your guiding light.

Practically speaking. Compassion does not mean giving the checking account to your child for unrestricted use. It also does not mean taking away privileges because your child got a bad report card.

Compassion means to process what occurred, think about why it possibly happened, analyze the pros and cons of what to do and then act nobly.

If one acts out compassion instead of any other emotion, the outcome will be the best it can be.

KABBALSITIC INSIGHTS

There is a famous anecdote recorded by the sixth Lubavitch Rebbe. When I was four years old, I asked my father: "Why did G-d make us with two eyes? Why not with one eye, just as they have one nose and one mouth?"

"Do you know the Hebrew alef-bet?" asked Father.

"Yes."

"Then you know that there are two very similar Hebrew letters, the shin and the sin. Can you tell the difference between them?"

"The shin has a dot on its right side while the sin is on its left,"

My father then said to me. "There are things which one must look upon with a right eye, with fondness and compassion, and there are things to be regarded with a left eye, with unimportance and disinterest.

On a siddur (prayerbook), one should look with the right eye. However, on a candy or toy, one should look with a left eye."

EFFECTIVE NON-CRITICISM

ADVICE THAT REALLY WORKS

There is a fellow I know, a Rabbi whose daughter was a heroin addict for many years. She is now married with a child and leads a very productive life. I met him a couple of weeks ago and asked him what he thought the reason was that his daughter got off drugs after many years and came back to a normal and fruitful life. What he shared with me was nothing less than brilliant, creative and dazzling.

He began by stating what was obvious to him, at least at his stage of his life, after having suffered tremendously. He claims that her road back to recovery started only when he and his wife stopped criticizing her. The way he said it was, "I stopped making her feel badly and instead I built up her self-worth."

I agree with him based on my experience that criticism is "poison for the soul," as it rots away at the inner fabric of the human regardless of age. When we criticize a person, even when we are doing it for their betterment, as we wish to guide/educate them to become a mensch, it is an error. Criticism is toxic to anyone's self- esteem. There are ways to get your message across without destroying your child's fragile infrastructure.

THE LETTER "I" TIMES THREE

The Rabbi suggested that we use the following approach when the need arises, instead of reprimanding, criticizing or rebuking someone. He also added that constructive criticism is an oxymoron as criticism is not constructive.

ONE: FIND "YOU" AND REPLACE WITH "I"

Do not make it personal.

Example. Instead of saying that "YOU did a hurtful thing by hitting your sister," replace it with, "I really feel badly when your sister gets hurt." One cannot argue with a feeling, and you are removing the pointed finger away from his face and instead pointing it at yourself.

TWO: TALK LOVE AND/OR PRIDE

Using the brother and sister example, "I know that you love me and would never want to hurt me." This is brilliant because the child knows that YOU know that he does love you and you are empowering him to stop whatever negative behavior he is doing. The same strategy can be used regarding pride when talking to an employee or student, etc.

THREE: MOVE ON

The last suggestion he gave me was to conclude with the following comment. "I know that in the future your sister will be protected." This accomplishes two things. 1. Not personalizing it as above. 2. You are moving on and looking to a better and brighter future, and are not belaboring the past.

I agree with every one of his three principles. I would, however, like to add just one more additional comment that helps me navigate interpersonal crisis.

I do not need to have the last word and I am more than content to let it go. True, I was not always this way, but as the world turns and I mature, I realize that while I may win the battle, I am also at risk of losing the war. Best be quiet until I am able to possibly get my point across not in the heat of the moment.

KABBALISTIC INSIGHTS

The Alter Rebbe, author of the Tanya/fundamental book on practical Mysticism expounds on the verse from the Torah, "You shall surely rebuke thy friend." He explains as follows, "rebuke should be used as a last option, and even then, you are only allowed to rebuke your friend. If the person is not at the friend level of relationship, then rebuking can cause more harm than could.

MARITAL INTIMACY

THE TWO WAYS OF AVOIDING PITFALLS

Please note I do not propose to excel at either parenting or marriage. I have just been doing both for so long that I now know where I need help. Many of the things I have written about are solely based on my experiences, how I have suffered colossal failures and learned to understand what I need to do better. I never want to sound preachy or condescending, but rather, I just have a passion to teach and then to learn as a student from the feedback.

Over the years as a congregational Rabbi, I find myself sitting across from couples both younger and older than myself in need of a third party to mediate some of the more thornier issues of marriage. And yes, over the years I have come to realize some very common patterns that are easily discernible when you analyze the picture from where I am sitting.

I find that the following two fundamentals in a marriage, if not nurtured properly, can cause even a great marriage to go stale quicker than Ezekiel bread left out on the counter in order to make French toast.

While it is true that there are hundreds of things that can go wrong including financial pressures, nervous breakdowns, long hours at work, tough kids, infidelity and so on, I still believe that most, if not all, can come under the heading of one of these two fundamentals.

The first item that allows mold to settle in between the former crazy lovebirds would be lack of intimacy. I am not referring to just the bedroom and that type of warm and intimate encounter. Sexual intimacy is paramount but it is only one part of what can be an incredible relationship. I am referring to simple intimate time spent together without the kids, job and all types of worry. Time alone without the kids is like chemotherapy for a toxic marriage as it zaps all the negative cells. Eating French toast together on the couch is hot and is just as therapeutic as a romp in the hay. Here are just some ideas that can bring your marriage alive and humanize you one to another: reading a book together, preparing a meal in the kitchen, sharing a few moments to catch up on your respective day and of course going out on the town for a pampered meal.

I know that many people feel that they can never spend that much time together as they have kids who need attention. I can assure you that spending special time with one's spouse once or twice a week will create way more harmony, healthy bodies and souls and greater family love than any homework help or mac & cheese you give your kids.

The second piece of advice I can give you comes straight from the Bible where it says, "A man shall leave his father and mother and cling to his wife." There are so many ways to look at what the Bible means by this. Does it mean that there is a Biblical obligation to move out of your parent's home? What are the millennials gonna do?

I believe that one of the lessons that the Bible is teaching is do not bring your whole family's idiosyncrasies into your house. Just because you saw and heard stuff in your home growing up - the way your mother treated your father or the way he yelled at the family - does not mean it is okay to continue your homebred bad habits. We are all victims and survivors of our upbringing in some way or fashion. What we need to learn is in the words of the famed Disney Princess …… LET IT GO. LET IT GO. Do not bring your garbage home from your upbringing. Just because your Pop was a yeller and had a sneer does not mean that it is okay for you to have one and do so as well.

This leads me to my next thought, which is really a continuation of the previous one.

When you come home at night to your house and you step over your homey threshold, leave all the day's putrid events at the front door in the mudroom where it belongs. You are married to your spouse and he/she is not married to your job, boss, coworkers, faux pas at work or office politics. Just as you do need to leave your parents' home, you also need to leave your work environment and enjoy the intimacy of a warm loving home.

KABBALISTIC INSIGHTS

One of the blessings that we recite under the chuppah at a wedding reads, "Grant abundant joy to these loving friends, as You bestowed gladness upon Your created being in the Garden of Eden of old."

What is the correlation between the newlyweds to the Garden of Eden? The answer is as follows. Adam and Eve did not have anyone else, they only had each other as no other human was created it. Therefore, when they "married" there was not an inkling of a doubt that perhaps there is someone more suited.

So, we bless these newlyweds that they should go into this marriage with a strong conviction, without doubt that they married the right person.

MARITAL PITFALLS

DREADED IN-LAWS

I have written on the concept of the Biblical command that when we get married we are obligated to leave our parents and cling to our spouses. We explained that we need to drop our bad habits from our upbringing and begin anew with the love of our life. We also clarified that the bottom line is that at the end of the day all that matters is you and your spouse and everything else can very well be noise and distraction.

There is another very important point to consider that I would be remiss if I did not bring up, especially as it is all too common. I am of course referring to the in-laws. There are probably not enough trees or enough ink material to pen or discuss this phenomenon. The "in-laws debacle" as I call it is responsible for more misery than the national debt and ISIS combined. The havoc is immense and the desired effect of getting one's daughter in-law, as an example, on board with how you see things never materializes.

The issue is really complex, particularly when it involves a (Jewish) son who loves his mother and also loves his wife, but the two loves do not get along with one another. How is a young man supposed to reconcile this conundrum? I believe this is what the Bible had in mind when it states, and this is verbatim, "A man shall leave his father and mother and cling to his wife." Buddy, there is no contest. When push comes to shove, one needs to place one's spouse on a pedestal EVEN at the expense of one's parents. If things can be worked out, then great. If not, one needs to leave the parents and cling to one's spouse. This is not an easy thing to accept and it is for precisely this reason the Torah had to say it.

When my eldest son was getting married, I called someone I respect to seek counsel, as I had never been in this capacity as a father in-law. Yet I, as a pulpit Rabbi, have seen firsthand the pitfalls of so many. The advice I received was priceless and my wife and I live by it. The sagely person told me in Yiddish that the best way to deal with an in-law is "ah farmachte moil un ah ofener keshener," which literally means, shut your mouth and open your wallet. Parents-in-law must never criticize, never antagonize and never push their opinion. At the same time, parents-in-law should take the kids out, buy them presents and be light and lively. Trust me when I tell you that one negative interaction with one daughter-in-law can negate hundreds of positive times.

The bottom line to all in-laws out there: Your sole job is to assure that your married children and their spouses are morally, emotionally and sometimes even financially supported. Your job is not to offer your advice and counsel, probably even when asked, unless it is really benign. Another wise person told me recently that he rarely gives his opinion on what his adult children should or should not be doing. He listens and then he says I know this great Rabbi, therapist or coach who can help you as he feels that he is not subjective enough to offer sound advice.

Lastly, to all married children out there: if your parent does offer up some criticism of your spouse, instead of creating the next world war, tell the offender that you really appreciate what he/she is trying to do but I need to ask you respectfully to back off and then forget about the conversation. Under no circumstances should you tell your spouse what your mother said. You dealt with it and it is over. As the Jewish adage states, "One is never allowed to tell a lie, however, one is not obligated to spew the whole truth."

KABBALISTIC INSIGHTS

There is a fascinating dialogue in the Torah. Abraham and Sarah were told that they were going to have a child. Sarah who was 90 at the time said to herself: "After I have withered will I get smooth skin, and my husband is old." When G-d repeated her comments to Abraham, he said that Sarah had said: "How can I give birth when I am old?"

We see from here that in order to maintain the peace, God changed Sarah's words from my husband is old to I am old.

LIFECYCLES

B.B.S.D – BAR/BAT MITZVAH STRESS DISORDER

The past few weeks I have been extremely busy officiating at Bar/Bat Mitzvah ceremonies. I simply love Bar & Bat Mitzvahs. There is no true pleasure a parent has than watching their child steal the show while he or she reads, sings and/or teaches valuable lessons. I as a parent have experienced this myself a few times with my own kids. I also love watching the parents and the grandparents who have tears in their eyes, kvelling to the brim. I also love seeing these children who came into my spiritual arms as a young child mature into someone with a voice, opinion and yes, sometimes attitude.

The Bar/Bat Mitzvah celebration is not solely a happy event though. There is so much stress and anxiety that goes into the planning and execution. I counsel many parents as how to lessen the Bar/Bat Mitzvah Stress Syndrome.

The following are my thoughts as to how to make this day more meaningful and way less stressful.

1. Enjoy the process. Whenever you feel overwhelmed and that there are so many moving parts that need to come together, pause, take a deep breath and smile. This is an incredibly happy occasion. Do not let your current negative inner voice distract you from the fact that you are about to celebrate a milestone in your child's life.

2. Don't be Bar/Bat Mitzvah centric. Remember that there is much more to Judaism than the Bar/Bat Mitzvah. Once you realize that the BM event is part of a cog in a wheel and not the whole car, you will be able to relax. It is not a life-or-death situation. It is simply an event.

3. For a few weeks before the big day make sure that you take your child to the Synagogue and stay with him or her for the duration or even a part of the service. Do not just drop them off and wave good bye. Show your children

135

that participation is very important to you and to your family, and not just a means to an end. By clearing your schedule of everything else you serve as a living example, that it not just about the Bar/Bat Mitzvah but rather part of growing up.

4. In addition, make sure that on every Friday evening, the family gathers around the table to enjoy a holy Shabbat meal, complete with good food, good wine, singing and plenty of laughter. Make this a non-negotiable item in your household. Tell the kids that they can go out before or after the special Shabbat meal but they must be present during. This is probably one of the most important things you can do as a parent (Jewish or not Jewish) is to have a mandatory set family time.

5. Lastly, I beg of you, do not spend exorbitant sums of money on a party. The attraction should not be the DJ, the cute dancers, centerpieces or the caterer, but rather the focus should be on the Soul of the Bar/Bat Mitzvah. There are plenty of charities that could use the money. When I hear of families that spend $40k-70k on a party for their 13-year-old kid, I need oxygen to push back the bile stuck in my throat. A couple of questions come to mind when I hear of this wastefulness. What if you took some of that coinage and went to Israel with the family in honor on this special holy day? Would it be so terrible if you took your child's besties to see a show and pizza instead of a $200 a head catered meal? This is true even if you are a family with financial means, let alone a family that has to go into hock to make this event happen. Don't do it.

As I mentioned above. Dedicate something to a not-for-profit. Make a donation to a charity and put up a plaque in his/her own honor. The Chai Center is a prime example of an organization that could use some shekels. www.thechaicenter.com/donate.

KABBALISTIC INSIGHTS

A Bar/Bat Mitzvah is not the end of someone's Jewish instruction and involvement. On the contrary it is just the beginning. In fact, this is the very reason we celebrate their big day. Until a child reaches the age of majority, there is no real obligation for a child to keep the mitzvahs. It is only after their Bar/Bat Mitzvah that they must.

We view the new Bar/Bat Mitzvah child as reinforcements that have now joined the Army of God.

THE BAR/BAT MITZVAH MISTAKE

FOCUS ON SELF

For those who know me personally and have heard me lecture previously, what I am about to write is nothing new. I feel though, that I cannot say or write it enough. The topic is entitled, "The Bar/Bat Mitzvah Mistake."

I have been wracking my brain to answer the following questions. Why is it that many of our Bar/Bat Mitzvah parents are so nervous about the big day that they will book the party years in advance, and painfully get into heavy debt making these few hours so special for their children that they can barely put gas into their car to get to the event?

Why do we rarely see these kids back in shul/temple post Bar/Bat Mitzvah? Most importantly, what can be done to assure that the Bar/Bat Mitzvah stays focused on Judaism and involved in the Jewish way of life once the great event has transpired and beyond? How can we best structure the Bar/Bat Mitzvah environment so that it will have a positive Jewish impact and effect for many years to come, especially through those turbulent college years?

After giving the above much thought, I realized that one answer would satisfy all of the above questions. The solution lies with the parents and not with the shul/temple. The respective Jewish organizations must take an active role in guiding the parents.

The following are my humble suggestions.

BRING YOUR CHILD TO SERVICES WITH YOU

Take your child to services and stay with him or her for the duration of the service. Do not just drop them off and wave goodbye and then go play tennis. Show your children that participation is very important to you and to your family, and not just a means to an end. By clearing your Shabbat schedule, or a part thereof, of everything else other than Jewish stuff will make you, the parent, a living example that in your life, God and Judaism are important and they come first. This holds just as true post Bar/Bat Mitzvah as well. Actions do speak louder than words.

SHOW POSITIVE JEWISH CHANGES

In honor of this most beautiful occasion of the Bar/Bat Mitzvah, you, as the parents, should encourage your entire family to take upon themselves an extra Mitzvah - good deed. Permit me to give you some examples. Mother and daughters should begin lighting the Shabbat candles and bring a spiritual warmth and light into the home on Friday nights. Dads should begin exploring the idea of putting on tefillin again one or two days a week. Even if you have not put on tefillin since your Bar Mitzvah, it is something you should do, as this will allow you to bond together in a very unique way.

TEFILLIN

It is my strong view that a Bar Mitzvah boy must own his very own pair of tefillin, not one on loan from his grandfather. Having one's own tefillin is something that the child will enjoy for a long time. It was bought for him and not just a "hand-me-down." If your child puts on tefillin, even occasionally, it is a very powerful tie to Judaism.

FRIDAY NIGHTS

Keep Friday nights sacrosanct. Make sure that on every Friday evening, the family gathers around the table and that kiddush is recited, and then is followed by a holy Shabbat meal, complete with good food, good wine, singing and plenty of laughter. If your kids wish to go somewhere Friday night, they should know that sitting with the family when they are home is non-negotiable.

$$$$$$$$$$$$$

Lastly, do not spend exorbitant sums of money on a party. The attraction should not be the DJ or the caterer, but rather the Soul of the Bar/Bat Mitzvah. There are plenty of charities that could use the money. The New York Friendship Circle, as an example, is a wonderful charity that I am involved with that helps children with special needs socialize and have friends and peers (www.nyfriendshipcircle.com/donate). Why waste it on a D.J. and dancers?

Teach your child that in his/her honor, donations were made and that children were helped. In the end, this is way more valuable than a cocktail hour.

KABBALISTIC INSIGHTS

Baal tashchis comes to mind when I think of all these exorbitant and ostentatious Bar/Bat Mitzvah parties. Baal tashchis means is needless destruction or waste is rooted in the Torah. Destroying, throwing out or ruining food, clothes, household goods, or anything else that could be useful to someone else is not approved of.

CREMATION CESSATION

NOT A JEWISH THING

As a Rabbi, I am obligated to teach since this is what the term Rabbi means. There is literally no end as to what can be taught. I have wanted to write about cremation for a long time now as it is becoming more and more common among Jews. What prompted me to write this now, even though I had something completely different to discuss, was yet another phone call on cremation.

I feel that I need to be direct, truthful, straightforward and frank as it is such an anathema to Judaism and Jewish sensibilities. This is especially so after so many Jews were cremated against their will by Hitler and the Nazi cohorts.

WHAT IS CREMATION?

Cremation is a method of body disposal that serves as an alternative to traditional burial. The remains are incinerated in an industrial furnace and reduced to basic chemical compounds. The entire cremation process takes roughly three hours to complete.

Once the remains are surrendered to the crematory, they are placed inside a cremation container. The container will then be placed inside the chamber, and the temperature is increased to approximately 1400°F to 1800°F. After a couple of hours, all organic matter will have been consumed by heat or evaporation.

The bone fragments that remain are carefully removed from the chamber, cleared of all metal components, then ground into fine particles that resemble ash but are much heavier (4–6 lbs) and are placed in a temporary container or an urn the family purchased.

WHAT IS WRONG WITH CREMATION?
BIBLICAL

There are various Jewish sources that discuss why we should be buried. The main one comes of course from the Torah that tells us to bury upon passing. The Torah mentions in a number of places that people were buried such as Sarah and Abraham as well as the other patriarchs and matriarchs and many others.

PHILOSOPHICAL

The philosophical reason is that our bodies do not belong to us. It is given to us on loan for the duration of our life on this earth. We are charged with looking after our body. Once our souls return to where they came from, we lose any rights to the body, and must return it as is. Can you imagine lending someone your cell phone to make a call and they then throw it on the floor and it is ruined.

ESOTERICAL

One of the central Jewish beliefs, as recorded by Maimonides, is that those who have passed away will be resurrected when the Messiah arrives. That means that their souls will return to their bodies and they will live again. The Jewish burial practices prepare the body for this experience.

KABBALISTICAL

The Kabbalah teaches that the soul of the departed remains hovering around the body at the funeral. It hears the eulogies, and sees those who have come to bid it a final farewell. After the burial, a part of the soul always remains at the gravesite. There they can be visited, and they are aware of and attentive to their visitors. Being cremated is unfair to the mourners. They cannot be expected to say farewell to an urn. They have no gravesite to visit and the soul has no resting place in this world.

PERSONAL

On more of a personal note, I recently spoke to someone who had their loved one cremated. This woman told me that she regrets it immensely. The service was extremely uncomfortable as friends and family came out of respect, but there was no casket, just an urn. In her words she said, "Try as I might, I was unable to make the association between my friend and the urn. There was no sense that honor was being paid to the departed - her presence was no longer felt."

PRACTICAL

Jewish law states that if someone is cremated by choice then the remains have no holiness and they are not allowed to be buried in a Jewish cemetery. Even if the person wills cremation, the wishes must be ignored. Unlike the bodily remains, there is no communal responsibility to care for the ashes. To quote Rabbi Moshe Feinstein, one of the greatest Jewish law authorities, "The cremated ashes may be thrown on the bridle path of Central Park."

Please share in the hopes we can get people to reevaluate and give this some more thought.

KABBALISTIC INSIGHTS

The body is on loan to us for the duration of our lives and beyond. It is not ours to do as we wish. We are merely the guardians.

It is for this reason that we are not allowed to tattoo, cut or afflict our body in any way. We are obligated to take care of ourselves both physically, emotionally and medically. There are many who argue that smoking is also forbidden.

A JEWISH FUNERAL – WHAT TO KNOW

A SHORT GUIDE TO PROTOCOL

Following up on my thoughts on cremation and how it is not allowed in Jewish Law, I was asked to write more on this topic. Truth be told, one can write a book on this subject matter, but due to time constraints, we will whet your appetite with small tidbits of information. Feedback and/or questions can be directed to my email at Rabbi@thechaicenter.com.

PRIOR TO DEATH

Jewish law is very clear here. If a person is about to pass on - we are talking really close - do not under any circumstances do anything to hasten the process. Because it may be your very action (like moving them), that hastens death.

Try to be in the room when the Soul leaves the body, as this is literally the last act you can do for the person while they are still alive. It is also meritorious for the Soul to know that the body will be taken care of.

POST PASSING

After saying the Shma Yisroel (Hear O Israel) prayer, close the eyes, straighten the hands and legs and call a Jewish funeral home to have them begin the process of removal.

One should strive to be present with the body (not always possible) until the funeral home comes, as it is important to have someone be near the body as a sign of respect.

WHAT MAKES IT A JEWISH FUNERAL

There are a few things during this process that make it a Jewish funeral as opposed to just a funeral. This list is not in order of any importance but just a list.

1. SHOMER: There should be someone sitting with the body from the time it arrives at the funeral home until burial. This is the most respectful thing you can do for the body which housed the holy Soul. Most people hire a service instead of doing it themselves. The shomer/watcher usually recites prayers from the Book of Psalms.

2. RITUAL WASHING/TAHARA: The body is always washed shortly before burial. If you choose not to have a Tahara for your loved one, then the funeral home will wash the body regardless (and charge you a washing fee) as this is the civil law. What is so special about the Tahara? Firstly, the body is washed by men for men and women for women. The washing is done with the utmost of respect and with the necessary prayers and protocols. In fact, after the process is over, the men or women ask for forgiveness from the body in case they did something disrespectful. The reason for the Tahara is essentially since the Soul is about to meet its maker, the body is prepared similarly as if going to a Mikvah.

3. SHROUDS: I always tell people that I do not like this word. It seems so creepy. Truth be told the shrouds are simply the following: linen shirt, linen pants, linen belt and linen hat. Essentially linen pajamas. This is exactly the garments that the high priests wore when they entered into the Holy of Holies once a year on the holiest day of the year, Yom Kippur. It is the penultimate clothes of purity.

4. WOODEN CASKET: The plainer the better as in a matter of hours it will be dinged and scratched. Do not spend thousands of dollars, as it is a complete waste of money. Instead of paying 18k on a casket, it will mean much more to the person who passed to give that money to charity (a plug for The Chai Center). However, any casket is fine as long as it does not contain any metal. All kosher wood caskets are made with wooden or liquid nails and contain no metal. The idea is that decomposition is part of repentance and metal does not decompose.

5. EMBALMING: This is completely not allowed, as it retards the decomposition process and it creates a complete sticky mess in the ground.

6. CREMATION: A big no no as well. See previous chapter.

7. OPEN CASKET: Once the person has had a Tahara, a ritual washing, the body should not be touched by anyone including family. The body is completely pure and ready for its most important meeting. Judaism does not believe in wakes or cosmetic touch ups post passing. In addition, we consider it disrespectful to look at a body that was once animated and is now bereft of soul, so we close the casket.

8. 72-HOUR TURNAROUND: In order for the Soul to continue its journey, the body must be buried in the ground as soon as possible. We do not delay burials. The only exceptions are as follows. A. To bury in Israel. B. To wait for the person's children to get into town. C. To bring the body in from out of state to be buried in a family plot. Even with children coming to town, we only wait up until 72 hours and not more. To delay strictly for the sake of delaying is frowned upon.

KABBALISTIC INSIGHTS

The reason as to why we strive to bury as quickly as possible, is because, when the soul leaves the body, before the body is buried, the soul is in a state of limbo.

The soul is neither animating the body nor can it begin its ascension to heaven as the body holds it back until burial is complete.

A JEWISH FUNERAL & SHIVA – WHAT TO KNOW

Last chapter we tackled what to do when someone passes away and the timeframe of when to do it in. In this piece, we will delve further and elaborate on the various customs and laws of a Jewish burial and Shiva practices. As always, questions are vital to knowledge, so feel free to ask at Rabbi@thechai-center.com.

PROCESSIONAL

The custom is to follow behind the hearse as it makes its way to the burial grounds. This is done as a sign of respect that this individual lived a life worth following. Once one gets to the burial plot, we do not run up to the grave but rather walk behind the casket once again as a sign of further respect. When we walk behind the casket, we recite prayers and we think positive thoughts about the person that passed.

DECEASED vs. PASSED

I personally never use the term deceased as I feel it is disrespectful. The term "deceased" implies cease to exist, when in fact, one can argue that the opposite is true. You see, when a person is alive and sickly, they are not fully present. They do not feel well, running to doctors and distracted from taking care of loved ones. When the Soul leaves the body, however, the Soul is no longer concerned about its own physical issues and can focus on family 24/7. In fact, even a healthy person is distracted by work, sleep and "Game of Thrones" episodes. So, I believe the term deceased is an incorrect and inappropriate term.

BURIAL

The Jewish view of burial is considered one of the greatest acts of kindness one can do for the person. The mitzvah of burial is called "chessed shel emes – kindness of truth," or in other words, true kindness. The reason it is given this term is because we bury our loved one strictly out of love and obligation and not because we have something further to gain from this individual. This person has passed on and can no longer give us a hug, money, a smile or cook a great meal.

There are four interesting uniquely Jewish practices that you should be aware of:

1. The first is that everyone is invited and encouraged to participate in this mitzvah. It may be a difficult thing emotionally, but it is a beautiful mitzvah to participate in.

2. In order to show that we are not eager to bury, and we prefer that this finality had not occurred, we purposefully turn the shovel backwards and then we awkwardly place earth on top of the casket. After a couple of shovels done backwards, we then continue to shovel normally.

3. Once we have finished shoveling, we do not hand the shovel to the next person, but rather, we place the shovel back into the earth and the next person then steps up to shovel. The reason for this custom is that we do not wish to appear overly eager to bury this individual.

4. Lastly, in order for the person to be considered properly buried, allowing the Soul to ascend, the casket needs to be fully covered with earth. You may have seen a burial where a symbolic shovel or two were placed over the grave. In truth, this is not enough to be considered a burial and should not be done. If the entire grave cavity can be filled that is even more worthwhile.

AFTER BURIAL

Once the burial is over by the filling in the grave or minimally covering the casket, Kaddish is said and forgiveness is asked of the person who passed so that the Soul can ascend without having any unfinished business with the family holding it back. The family then leaves the cemetery by walking in between a line of well-wishers who comfort them.

KADDISH/MEMORIAL PRAYER

Kaddish should be said three times a day for 11 months in the context of a minyan (quorum). Kaddish is said to help elevate the Soul. If the family is not able to commit to saying kaddish for the 11 months, then I recommend hiring a service. This is exactly what I did when my father passed and I was concerned that I would miss. The organization I used was www.MemorialKaddish.com.

SHIVA

The Shiva house and Shiva in general is designed to help the family grieve and to talk about their loved one. Many Shiva houses that I have witnessed have turned into a party house complete with pastrami and scotch. This misses the whole point and it also creates a hardship for the family to have to provide platters of food and cleaning personnel. When you go to a Shiva house, inquire about their loved ones, don't shy away from talking about the passing, etc. Cold cuts will not help them mourn, but talking about the newly departed will.

KABBALISTIC INSIGHTS

The Kabbalah shares that the Soul (part thereof) of the recent departed returns to the home where it lived and remains there for the duration of Shiva. When we hold prayers and recite Psalms, the soul finds comfort.

The soul is not physical and is therefore not affected by physical phenomenon. The soul can be in heaven and in a body and is no contradiction.

A DEATH WITH MEANING

SCHOOLED BY A 19-YEAR-OLD

This past weekend was one that will stay with me forever. It was painful emotionally, challenged me physically, and shook my faith. Yet, it was ironically inspiring.

On Saturday night, I received a text from my dearest lifelong friends that their daughter was involved in a car accident and she was in the hospital some 450 plus miles away. There were no flights available, so we decided to drive to Buffalo. The three of us drove together. Well more accurately, dad drove and I was charged with getting information and pushing for the best care. At that time, we had no idea what we were facing. We just prayed and hoped that everything would be ok.

When we got there, it was somewhat clear that this was a bad accident and we may need a miracle. I say "may" because we were very optimistic and positive and still hoped that she would just naturally heal from her injuries. The parents did not give up hope for a moment. Their strength of courage and conviction rendered me speechless.

The parents cautioned the entire angelic ICU staff with a pointed finger and a stern gaze that they too must never give up hope. At first, one of the doctors began to state that the situation is dire, but after listening to the dad, she was so inspired that she doubled and redoubled the efforts of the whole staff.

There was not one stone left unturned. The ICU staff at Erie County Medical Center are heroes in my eyes. They literally spent every second of the 20 hours that she was in their unit at her bedside. They were behind her every step of the way, believing and praying for this 19-year-old girl. I witnessed one of the staff members saying a prayer with her head bowed. Even the person who emptied the wastebasket paused at the entrance to the room where Dina lay and watched mom and dad saying the Tehillim/Psalms with tears in her eyes.

Dina herself fought valiantly. While most people in her condition would have succumbed to their injuries within a very short time, Dina did not. She held on for close to 24 hours, which the staff told me was nothing short of a miracle in itself. What I learned about her while standing in the room with her was that she was a warrior filled with valor and courage. What she taught me as her life ebbed away is that you must never give up. It may not end the way you want it to, but still, you need to do your part.

Judaism has a belief system that every moment your soul is in your body is precious and should not be held lightly. Every hour is like a lifetime and should be spent when awake accomplishing at maximum capacity.

Well, Dina Leah excelled in her last 24 hours at just that. She taught us all the value of life. She schooled us in strength. She made us believers in an impossible situation.

The local Shluchim/Emissaries, Rabbis Gurary and Labkowski, came right on over with Kosher food in one hand, while on the phone talking to the various doctors that they personally knew in the other, to assure that everything possible was being done. The staff took this all in, saw the commitment to strangers, and were honored to be part of Dina's team.

Dina Leah, thank you for your life's lessons. I know that you will continue to fight for your mom, dad and family. I will always remember your dazzling smile. Most importantly, I will never forget what you taught me while we shared some very special moments together in an austere room in Buffalo. I draw strength from you and will never forget your life lessons. Your entire family are proud of you and they miss you very much.

Thank you for being you.

KABBALISTIC INSIGHTS

When a person passes young, it is not just luck of the draw. The Baal Shem Tov related that it is a special, lofty and unique soul that needed to come down. Either, the soul just needs a short time here to fulfill its mission which usually can take a lifetime, or it comes down to share its light because someone needed help.

REFLECTIONS OF A LOVED ONE

A SYMBIOTIC RELATIONSHIP

My father's third yahrzeit/anniversary of passing was recently observed, and I find myself ruminating about him in particular and loss/passing in general.

We are taught that on a yahrzeit, one needs to think about the individual's contribution to humanity and family. In other words, an anniversary of passing should not be just another ordinary day of the week, but rather a day filled with reflection of what lessons one has learned from the individual whose yahrzeit one is commemorating, and then a dosage of introspection of self as to how to implement those lessons.

DECEASED vs. PASSED

As a general rule, I do not use the term deceased as it implies cease to exist, which to me, means over, kaput, finished and done with. In fact, I would argue that the person's energy, aspirations and wishes exist more than they did while the Soul was enmeshed in a physical body, as the physical person has many corporeal needs such as sleep, food and livelihood (or golf when retired). The Soul that is not bound in a physical form on the other hand, can just focus on the relationship it has with its family with little to no distractions.

If this is true on a regular day, then it is especially true on a yahrzeit where the Kabbalah teaches that all the spiritual achievements of one's life - including every positive thought, word, or deed -radiate and are revealed in the world and in the Heavens on the day of the Yahrzeit.

This approach underlines the basic view of Judaism that, in reality, there is no "death" in matters of Godines. The physical body is buried in the ground as it is mortal, but the Soul, which is immortal as it is a spark of Godines, is eternal and the term death does not apply to anything eternal. Rather, the Yahrzeit, and even the very day of passing, represents a transition or a passing, but certainly not a death.

THE IMPORTANCE OF YAHRZEIT

We are taught that Spirituality can and does influence our physical world and vice versa. Therefore, it is readily apparent to understand that relatives of the person who passed can benefit each other in a spiritual symbiotic relationship. The Soul implores God to take good care of its family who are still living in this physical and corporeal world, and we in turn help elevate the Soul to new heights. This is especially true on a yahrzeit. On this day, every Mitzvah performed and every effort to improve one's spiritual life brings great merit to the deceased. This is especially true for one's father and mother.

MIXED FEELINGS

On one hand, we learn from our sages that the Soul of the departed rises from one spiritual world to a higher one. This is what we mean when we say, "May the Neshoma/Soul of your loved one have an aliya." It is therefore a day where we celebrate the fact that the Soul has attained new heights in the heavenly realms. On the other hand, the Yahrzeit and the heavenly elevation emphasizes the loss sustained by the family, which results in a feeling of emptiness and contemplation.

RECIPROCAL ENERGY

During this day, one should work to align one's life on this earth to the path followed by the Soul above, which is constantly on the ascent. Meaning, just as the Soul continuously rises year after year, going from strength to strength, so must those associated with the Soul steadily rise in their advancement in doing good deeds and being a better person.

Interestingly enough, it actually works something like this. When a child/relative performs a good deed in honor of their loved one, the Soul then gets rewarded by Hashem/God and is elevated to higher spiritual loftiness, which in turn allows the Soul more leverage in imploring Hashem/God to help their loved ones in need. It is a positive cycle of good.

SOME JEWISH CUSTOMS OF YAHRZEIT

1. On the eve of the Yahrzeit, each mourner kindles a candle that should remain lit for the entire twenty-four-hour period.

2. Some take it upon themselves to fast on the day of the Yahrzeit. Most do not. I cannot even if I wanted to as the Yahrzeit falls out during the holiday of Sukkot when it is forbidden to fast.

3. If possible, a son should lead all the prayer services of the Yahrzeit day. If one does not lead the services, one should at least pray with a Minyan

(quorum of ten Jewish males over age thirteen) and recite the Mourner's Kaddish at the designated times during the service.

4. One kindles five candles for each level of the departed's Souls on the prayer leader's stand in the synagogue when leading the prayer services.

5. Many study Mishnayot (Mishnaic laws) in honor of the Soul, especially the chapters that begin with the letters of the Hebrew name of the departed.

6. Some visit the gravesite on this day to recite prayers and Psalms.

KABBALISTIC INSIGHTS

The Soul always remains attached to its family, and the relationship is never severed. We are taught the soul laughs when we do and cries when we cry. There is a custom to bring an invitation (wedding/bar mitzvah/) to the grave of a loved one. Invite them and they will be in attendance. Don't tell the caterer.

THE LAST KADDISH

I remember the day I stopped saying kaddish for my father. It was on a Wednesday evening, the 11th month milestone of my father's passing that I stopped saying the kaddish prayer that I had done so religiously three times a day in the context of a Minyan at a shul during services. While preparing for the last Kaddish I had a fleeting thought. What now? For 11 months I was focused on my father. Every day I was doing something tangible in his honor and memory, and now that this period is over, where does it leave me/him?

I had no quick answer that resonated with me that night, but the following morning I started pondering again. What I realized was that the last Kaddish was not a somber goodbye to dad, but rather, a cheerful hello.

You see, one of the reasons we say Kaddish for the 11 months is because the Soul goes through a transition upon passing that can last for 11 months. During this transition the Soul is extremely busy with getting to "know the ropes" of heaven and settling into a new routine. During this time, the Soul cannot focus its time on its family due to its preoccupation. Now that the 11 months are up, and the Soul is comfortably entrenched and has found its niche, it can now focus on its family.

My father is now reunited with me and the rest of the famjam. My Kaddish is now over; it is a little surreal but the true and deep connection is only just beginning.

Welcome back Dad.

KABBALISTIC INSIGHTS

The Kaddish prayer does not mention death or dying at all. It speaks about God's greatness and asks for God to usher in the messianic era, and end all suffering and distress.

It is very easy to reach out to God when you have just won the lottery. How about when a parent just passed? Reciting Kaddish is an affirmation of your belief in God even in the most trying of times.

JEWISH AND OTHER SPECIAL DAYS

AVOID THE HOLIDAY RUSH

PRAY EARLY

The High Holidays begin with Rosh Hashana and culminates with the Shofar blast during the Neila (5th and final prayer) prayer on Yom Kippur. During these 10 days, most Jews feel the importance of connecting with their Creator and implore Him to bestow on us shelter and protection, to give and forgive, and health and wealth, etc. What is lesser known is that the month before, beginning 30 days prior; we begin our supplication to God, as we do not want to show up unprepared on the big day.

Important to point out that these 30 days of preparation are extremely vital to the High Holidays themselves, and not just a good idea to prepare.

The Jewish month prior to the High Holidays is called ELUL. During this month, there are three beautiful customs that come to mind to help us prepare.

The first is to hear a synopsis of the notes of the Shofar being blown. The cry of the Shofar represents our deep inner voice. When we awaken this voice, it immediately sets us on the track of introspection (panic that Rosh Hashanah is coming. Where do I get raisin challah?)

The second is to increase our charity. The Kabbalah as well as the Talmud state that when one is benevolent to others, God will respond in kind and be benevolent in return.

The last custom is to recite chapter 27 of Psalms every day. This Psalm teaches us: that as Jews we are to hope in God; and then we are to do everything we can to strengthen ourselves as if we were wholly left to our own fates;

and then we are to continue to hope in Him despite having acted as if we were wholly on our own.

I have included the Psalm.

27:1 The LORD is my light and my salvation; whom shall I fear? The LORD is the strength of my life; of whom shall I be afraid?

27:2 When the wicked, even mine enemies and my foes, came upon me to eat up my flesh, they stumbled and fell.

27:3 Though a host should encamp against me, my heart shall not fear: though war should rise against me, in this will I be confident.

27:4 One thing have I desired of the LORD, that will I seek after; that I may dwell in the house of the LORD all the days of my life, to behold the beauty of the LORD, and to enquire in his temple.

27:5 For in the time of trouble he shall hide me in his pavilion: in the secret of his tabernacle shall he hide me; he shall set me up upon a rock.

27:6 And now shall mine head be lifted up above mine enemies round about me: therefore will I offer in his tabernacle sacrifices of joy; I will sing, yea, I will sing praises unto the LORD.

27:7 Hear, O LORD, when I cry with my voice: have mercy also upon me, and answer me.

27:8 When thou said, Seek ye my face; my heart said unto thee, Thy face, LORD, will I seek.

27:9 Hide not thy face far from me; put not thy servant away in anger: thou hast been my help; leave me not, neither forsake me, O God of my salvation.

27:10 When my father and my mother forsake me, then the LORD will take me up.

27:11 Teach me thy way, O LORD, and lead me in a plain path, because of mine enemies.

27:12 Deliver me not over unto the will of mine enemies: for false witnesses are risen up against me, and such as breathe out cruelty.

27:13 I had fainted, unless I had believed to see the goodness of the LORD in the land of the living.

27:14 Wait on the LORD: be of good courage, and he shall strengthen thine heart: wait, I say, on the LORD.

SHANA TOVA

KABBALISTIC INSIGHTS

The third Lubavitcher Rebbe once said that if we only knew the power of Psalms and the effects, we would recite them constantly. "Know that the chapters of Psalms shatter all barriers, they ascend higher and still higher with no interference; they prostrate themselves in supplication before the Master of all worlds, and they effect and accomplish with kindness and compassion."

CUSTOMIZED NEW YEAR PRAYERS

ONE SIZE DOES NOT FIT ALL

As the High Holidays are just around the corner, we are taught that it is prudent to start getting our thoughts in order so that Rosh Hashana does not become Rush Hashana. There are many themes on Rosh Hashana. One of them is that it is a propitious time to ask God for help and guidance in the upcoming New Year.

While it is true that there is a special High Holiday Prayer book called a Machzor, which arrange our prayers for us, nothing can compare, however, to our own individualized and customized prayer that we lay out for ourselves and our own particular and specific needs. Just as there are no two fingerprints alike, so too there are different and definite needs that we all have.

Once Labor Day passes, I begin reflecting on what I would ask for and what assistance I need. The following is my preliminary contemplation and I am sharing this to help you get your own Soul searching happening.

NOT LOOKING BACK

Almighty God,

Thank you for sustaining me for yet another year. While this past year has been a difficult one personally, communally and globally, I will not dwell on it as it is past, over, gone and finished. You gave us eyes only in the front of our head and not also in the back, to teach us that we must only look forward and not live in the past. I do hope that having said this, I would have learned from my past mistakes in order to recognize what not to repeat in the future.

FAMILY. (PLEASE ADD SPECIFIC NAMES & DETAILS)

I pray that this coming year my children are happy and healthy and that they struggle with only small obstacles. Please fulfill their positive wishes and aspirations and guide them on their respective paths to maturity and stability. I ask that my wife and I be given the strength and wisdom to be able to be there for them, undistracted, and that pride and joy be in abundance. Please give us the tools to be able to help them when needed. Please bless our respective siblings and their extended families.

LIVELIHOOD

I ask that you once again provide a modest living so that my family and I do not become a burden on anyone. I request that any monies I do earn be through dignified means. I do affirm that I believe that I cannot earn a penny more than you have blessed me with. At the same time, I do understand that I need to make myself a receptacle for blessings by doing my part.

MY GOVERNMENT

Please endow all branches of government with a positive disposition towards the Jewish people. Do not allow a few anti-Semites to poison the other lawmakers. Bestow on the three branches of government the ability to make right and moral decisions so that this country can truly remain the blessed United States. Heal our divisions and allow all its citizens and residents to come together for the common good. Protect these shores from those who seek to destroy. Help our government through the challenge of accepting immigrants, while at the same time keeping us safe. Guide them toward peace and never war.

MY COMMUNITY

As a Rabbi, I am responsible for the community I reside in and serve. I urge God's blessing to rest on all of us to be healed from our wounds, whether physical, mental or spiritual. Help them with clarity of thought and peace of mind. Give them what they need and free them from nonsense burdens so that they can be free to devote time to doing acts of kindness and caring. Inspire them to continue making good decisions.

ISRAEL

Please protect her from her multiple enemies from within and beyond her borders. Keep her morally strong and do not allow her agitators to weaken her integrity. Allow Israel to spread her goodness and ingenuity to all the world. Give her leaders the wisdom to be able to communicate effectively with her neighbors. Protect the citizens from murdering thugs who have been misguided and manipulated by evil people.

KABBALISTIC INSIGHTS

There is a story told about a farmer boy who was illiterate and could not pray. He went to Synagogue on Yom Kippur where he felt the intensity of the Congregation. The boy was overcome with emotion and at the top of his lungs he shouted "Cock-a-doodle-do! G-d, have mercy!"

The Baal Shemtov who was there commented that this boy's prayers pierced the heavens due to its pureness and sincerity.

ROSH (NOT) RUSH HASHANAH

BE PREPARED

It is unbelievable that Rosh Hashanah is literally just a few days away. Everyone is shopping for round challahs, honey, pomegranates and a new designer mask. With dressing rooms now open at the mall, we are running to buy new outfits and shoes. All fine and dandy and very appropriate.

However, one critical ingredient cannot be overlooked, what to pray for on this Rosh Hashanah? We need to be prepared and organized so that when we open the prayer book, whether at home or in shul, one must absolutely identify what it is that we are asking for. If we only start thinking about the most important aspect of Rosh Hashanah, it will feel rushed and hence the name Rush Hashanah.

The following is what I believe to be universal needs, wishes and wants, so therefore applicable to everyone.

HEALTH

Health is critical. Any person struggling with real health concerns (like men with a common cold), can tell you that it is overriding and prevailing. It literally trumps all other concerns and issues. In fact, it makes most other worries and fears look trivial compared to health. The body is very complex and while the medical and scientific community have made huge strides, they still have a long way to go. Take COVID-19 as an example of something that has baffled virologists and other experts.

Therefore, while we put our trust in doctors, nurses and specialists, we must put our faith and belief in a higher power. We should pray this Rosh Hashanah that we have good bodily health, plain and simple without compromise.

CHILDREN

The Talmud states that rearing is extremely difficult, and it is. To know when to discipline or coddle one's child takes great Solomonic–like wisdom. I once heard someone say that "disciplining children is like holding a wet bar of soap. A grip that is too firm or one that is too gentle will cause the bar of soap – or a child – to slip through your hands." We need to ask for divine guidance to know when to hold and when to fold them. When do you look away and when must you not look away?

I once met a man while I was engaged to be married and he told me that he is the parent of 10 kids. I asked him how he manages to love and discipline them. His response was that he attributes his success with having good kids as 10 percent from he and his wife and 90 percent from above.

SHOLOM BAYIS – DOMESTIC HARMONY

The way I see it there are two types of love. Parents, by nature love their child(ren). From the moment the child is conceived there is this extreme love. Then there is the love between husband and wife. It was born long after this man and woman were born. And, therefore, no matter how intense the love, it fades over time. No marriage has ever survived on passion and love alone. The Hollywood claim that this may be the case has destroyed many a marriage. Maintaining a successful and harmonious marriage involves work, commitment and dedication. It also takes a cargo boatload of patience, wisdom and discretion - when to say something, when to keep quiet, etc. Once again, we need divine assistance to navigate the turbulent waters of spousal war and peace.

FINANCIAL SUCCESS

Everyone has a different definition of what it means to be successful. Some are not satisfied until they own vacation homes on three continents. Others collect rare cars, while others go nowhere and do not own a car, but do own real estate in midtown Manhattan. So, what financial success should we be praying for? Judaism teaches us that it is a beautiful blessing from above to become wealthy as long as it does not affect who you are.

I heard a story when I was a child about a regular hard-working man who earned a decent living and gave 10 percent to charity. He was reliable and consistent. Then the strangest thing happened. The moment his business became lucrative, he eased up on his charity. It seemed the more money he made, the less he helped others. This went on for a while until his Rabbi intervened and taught him a very profound lesson. The Rabbi took him to a window that was completely transparent and showed him the street below. He then showed him a mirror that reflects the viewers face and is not transparent. The

Rabbi explained that the window and the mirror are both made of glass. The only difference would be the silver backing behind the glass. The businessman understood the metaphor that a little silver caused him to only see himself.

It is okay to make a verbal contract with God during your prayers. Help me be successful so that I can take care of my family, and I promise to take care of your family.

May we all be blessed with health, happiness, exquisite joy from our children, peace of mind, peace at home and the world over.

KABBALISTIC INSIGHT

It is a known fact that Chassidim have a reputation of being late. I am not sure of its origin. I am not even sure if it is in fact true. I do know that the Lubavitcher Rebbe was never late for any services or lectures.

I do recall one episode when the Rebbe was late for services, and it was explained that there was this young woman who was very sick and in hospital, and he was promised an update which was late in coming.

SOUNDS OF SILENCE

NOISE CURFEW
SILENCE IN TURKEY

A few years ago, I remember reading about a Turkish fellow who made quite an impact in Istanbul when he became internationally known as "The Standing Man" by standing quietly in Istanbul's Taksim Square in a silent protest against Tayyip Erdogan.

SILENCE IN SEATTLE

Then, a couple of months ago, tens of thousands of marchers, some report as high as 60,000, protested silently in the streets of Seattle to oppose police brutality. It was so effective that hundreds of businesses closed in solidarity with the marchers.

SILENCE IN THE TOWN OF HUNTINGTON

Recently, the Town of Huntington officials voted to tighten the use of gas-powered leaf blowers due to noise and other health concerns. No noise after 6 PM they ruled.

JEWISH SILENCE

This got me thinking about silence.

In a few days, Rosh Hashanah, the Jewish New Year will begin. In contradistinction to the civil New Year, there is no music, champagne, disco party, party horns or streamers. Instead, we will be gathered together in the synagogue (or at home) silently reading the various pieces of liturgy praying for a healthy (read COVID-19-free), happy (read COVID-19-free), and successful (read COVID-19- free) New Year. The most intense and powerful time of prayers, where we ask personally for an abundance of mercy and goodness, is when we are praying the silent "Amidah," a prayer that is said under our breath, only audible to our ears whilst standing in awe of the New Year and what it will bring.

In one of the oldest Jewish books that we have, the Mishna, there is a quote attributed to Rabbi Shimon son of Rabbi Gamliel that says, "During my entire life, I grew up among the scholars, and I never found anything better for the physical body than silence." WHY? Why would one of the greatest

Rabbis suggest that silence is a value worth pursuing? Isn't silence the absence of speech?

WHY SILENCE

Why all this silence? After all, we are human beings who have been blessed with the power of speech. In this respect, we are different from all other creations in that we speak and communicate to one another with full cogent sentences. So, is praying silently so important and how come the largest protest in Seattle's history, which was silent, was so effective?

TYPES OF SILENCE

I believe the answer lies in understanding that there is not just one type of silence but rather a few. You see silence can be simply when there are no words, or silence is when there are words but we nonetheless choose to be silent. In addition, there is a bad silence (married people know what I am talking about), but there is a greater silence, one of connection. One type of silence can be completely non-effective while the other extremely effective.

BAD SILENCE

The first silence we will analyze is completely negative and is essentially an inability or unwillingness to communicate effectively. This silence causes division and separation, creating dysfunction in human relationships. An example of bad silence would be giving someone the silent treatment. When we are offended or hurt, respectful conversation is the best way to resolve conflict and repair relationships. Keeping silent and refusing to talk is a form of aggression, and possibly even abuse, and totally and completely ineffective.

SAD SILENCE

There is another harmful silence and that is when someone is verbally or physically abusive and the receiver of the abuse is too afraid to speak up and is therefore silent. To this person, I say there is help, and you need to be silent no longer.

GOOD SILENCE

The next category of silence is a good silence. One that is positive, constructive and creates connectivity. True communication occurs when there is a willingness to have mutual understanding and deep respect for each other's position. This is where appropriate silence can be very effective, as our words must be well thought out before we speak.

An example of good silence would be rather than responding impulsively to one's spouse, we wait and think it through and only after this contemplation, do we reply. When your mother told you to think before you speak, it was not a suggestion or optional. She was teaching you a real-life lesson.

Another great illustration would be to actively listen to someone else without interrupting them. This will allow you to really understand where they are coming from. The person speaking will draw much comfort from knowing that they are being heard and not just dismissed.

SAGE ADVICE

It is this kind of silence that Rabbi Shimon is referring too. Being silent does not necessarily mean not to communicate. On the contrary, silence, when done right, is the perfect way of respectful communication.

We do not always need to talk to be heard. Before we can be good communicators, we must learn the art of good silence.

Hmmm. How does this all fit in with silence of the lambs?

KABBALISTIC INSIGHT

The holy Vishnitzer Rebbe once told a person that "Our sages say that just as it is a mitzvah to speak out when you will be listened to, so it is a mitzvah to not say anything when you know you will not be listened to."

"But what does it mean to not say anything?" the Rebbe continued. "You have to go to the person to whom you are not supposed to say what he won't listen to, and then face-to-face not say it!"

PRAYING FOR A BETTER YEAR

PUSHING THE RESTART BUTTON
THE FIRST TWO AND A HALF MONTHS OF 2020

We all know and recognize that 2020 has been a year of extreme anxiety and difficulty. The spaghetti hit the fan in early January when brush fires destroyed millions of acres of land in Australia, then Kobe Bryant and others were killed in an accident. February and March were no better with the impeachment debacle and the insane Netflix series "Tiger King," featuring Carole Baskin and Joe Exotic. This mini-series took us all down a few intellectual notches.

MARCH THROUGH AUGUST 2020

Then in mid-March came the ultimate plague, the Coronavirus or COVID-19. Life stopped as we know it. So much sickness and death. NBA cancelled the rest of the season. The Tokyo Olympics were pushed to 2021 and schools closed, houses of worship were shuttered, restaurants were relegated to only take out and then all workers, except for essential employees, had to stay home.

Then to add to our troubles, George Floyd was brutally killed, leading to protests in the streets objecting to police brutality. Sadly, opportunists took advantage and looted stores and shops, and rioters/anarchists shaking off their COVID-19 blues went to work on what they do best. It was, and still is, insanity.

When will this all end? When can we get back to normal?

Most people have written off 2020 as the year of Gehenna and cannot wait until the calendar turns the page to 2021.

I have not.

ROSH HASHANAH 2020 OR 5781

As far as the Jewish calendar is concerned, everything begins anew on Rosh Hashanah, the very first day of the Jewish New Year. This year Rosh Hashanah begins Friday night, September 18.

What we believe is that the whole world is viewed and judged with a new spirit on Rosh Hashanah, completely unlike any other year. Last Rosh

Hashanah was clearly one when it was decided that the year ahead would be a challenging one (even throwing in killer hornets). But now, thankfully, I might add, the year is soon to be over.

This Rosh Hashanah we have an opportunity to reverse this negative trend we have been experiencing these past few months. This is a unique moment in time when we can beseech the heavens to take away the sickness, madness, worry, apprehension and uneasiness. We need to be clear that COVID-19, with all its ramifications, cannot go on. It must stop. We need to rebuild our esteem, lives, homes and businesses.

EYES FORWARD

Judaism teaches us that we are designed with eyes in the front of our face and not in the back. If you think about it, having an eye in the back of your head would be really valuable, especially when it comes to parallel parking. The reason why we are fashioned this way is to teach us that we must look forward to the future and not constantly look back. In fact, the only time we should look back is to learn from our mistakes. However, all things being equal, we are only to look forward.

WHY WE SHOULD PRAY

I plan to offer a special COVID-19 prayer this Rosh Hashanah, together with all my other prayers and good resolutions. I recognize that prayer is the very underpinning or foundation, if you will, of our lives. A prayer should never be taken lightly. Prayer is the language of the soul in conversation with God. Judah Halevi, the great 11th-century poet, said that prayer is to the soul what food is to the body. Without prayer, something within us atrophies and dies. It is possible to have a life without prayer, just as it is possible to have a life without music, or love, or laughter, but it is a diminished thing, missing whole dimensions of experience.

WHAT SHOULD WE PRAY?

The following is my unique prayer for the New Year.

On this holy day of Rosh Hashanah, I, Yakov, the son of Shterna Sarah, offer the following prayer.

We live in unprecedented times.

There have been over 180,000 recorded deaths from COVID-19.

There is so much sickness, pain, suffering, unhappiness and emotional trauma.

There is shamefully a great division in our country, where voices are raised and tempers flare.

There is such uncertainty – which is causing more uncertainty.

We need help.

For all who have contracted COVID-19, we pray for your care and a speedy healing.

For those who are vulnerable, we pray for safety and protection.

For all who experience fear or anxiety, we pray for peace of mind.

For our fellow citizens and residents, we pray that we regain respect for one another.

For public officials and politicians, we pray for wisdom and guidance.

May the Jewish year of 5781 be the polar opposite of the previous one.

The above is just a suggestion. Please feel free to use or draft your own.

Blessed be the New Year.

KABBALISTIC INSIGHTS

There is a profound reason as to why the new year is called Rosh Hashanah, which means Head of the year and not Techilas Hashana, which means beginning of the year.

The head is control. Within the head lies the motherboard where everything the body does from talking to walking, from seeing to seething takes place.

The lesson is that we need to take charge at the beginning of the year to assure we do the right thing. Be in control of your emotions. Be in control of your cravings, etc.

RBG AND YOM KIPPUR

A STORY OF COURAGE

On Rosh Hashanah 2020, Justice Ruth Bader Ginsburg returned her soul to her maker. This courageous woman was known not only for her intellect, but also for her convictions.

RBG accepted an offer to teach at Columbia in 1972, where she became the first female professor at Columbia to earn tenure. Ginsburg also directed the influential Women's Rights Project of the American Civil Liberties Union during the 1970s. In this position, she led the fight against gender discrimination and successfully argued six landmark cases before the U.S. Supreme Court. Ginsburg took a broad look at gender discrimination, fighting not just for the women left behind, but for the men who were discriminated against as well.

She was appointed to the U.S Supreme Court where she made great strides in improving the lives of those who were discriminated against. I recently read a story about her that displays both her morals and courage. It is about Yom Kippur which begins this coming Sunday night.

This story was told by Paul Hamburger, a prominent attorney in Washington DC and part of the Chabad community in Potomac, and a member of the Chabad on Campus National board.

Mr. Hamburger relates the following:

"Last fall, I attended a dinner program at the U.S. Supreme Court building for which Justice Ruth Bader Ginsburg was our host. During her remarks and in an off-hand comment, Justice Ginsburg pointed out that the U.S. Supreme Court always opens its sessions on the first Monday in October; but this year, because Rosh Hashanah fell on Monday, they would not hear arguments in cases until Tuesday.

To appreciate the significance of that statement, you need to know that since 1975, there has been a federal law mandating that the Court open its session on the first Monday in October. So how was it that they moved the date for oral argument? The Supreme Court is steeped in its traditions and, obviously, if any institution is going to follow the law, it would be the U.S. Supreme Court.

The precedent for this change of date was from 2003. Then, for the first time in the 28 years since the 1975 law, the Court officially moved its opening arguments from the first Monday in October (which was Yom Kippur in 2003) to the next Tuesday. So, it has happened before that the Court officially moved the date for oral argument in deference to the High Holy Days on the Jewish calendar.

We know THAT it happened; but HOW did it happen?

I decided to ask Justice Ginsburg. After she sat at her place at the dinner, I sat next to her and asked her how the decision was made. In response to my question, she perked up and told me the story. "Several years ago," she began, "Yom Kippur fell on the first Monday in October.

Justice Breyer and I went to the Chief Justice [Justice Rehnquist] and pointed that out. We said that the Court should delay the opening in deference to the holiday. The Chief was not persuaded. He said 'Why should we delay? We always hold our Friday conferences on Friday, even if it is Good Friday.' So, I replied to him 'So move that conference to Thursday; that would be fine for us.' The Chief was still not persuaded. Do you know what persuaded him?" she asked, looking right at me. "I explained to him that lawyers wait their entire career to appear before the Supreme Court. For many of them, it is a once in a lifetime chance to argue in the Supreme Court. What if a Jewish lawyer wanted to appear in court? We should not make that lawyer choose between observing his or her faith and appearing before the Court. That persuaded him and we changed the calendar."

I would say that Justice Ginsburg did more than just change the Court's calendar.

When Sandy Koufax (in 1965) refused to pitch in the World Series in deference to Yom Kippur; that was a courageous act and statement of faith.

Following that example, Justice Ginsburg could have said "Go ahead and hold the oral arguments; but I won't go because it is Yom Kippur." But she did not do that. Even Sandy Koufax did not make them move the date for the World Series. Justice Ginsburg moved the date for the legal equivalent of the World Series.

Another important part of Justice Ginsburg's act was that the argument that persuaded the Chief Justice was not based on the needs of a specific lawyer who was arguing a specific case. It was an argument on behalf of all Jewish lawyers who then existed or may exist in the future; it was an argument based on the possibility that there might be a Jewish lawyer at some point in time who would need to appear before the Court and not be comfortable choosing between his or her faith and the pinnacle of a legal career. Therefore, the precedent was set that even the statutory First Monday in October could be set aside.

A true story of strength and courage.

KABBALISTIC INSIGHTS

In the mystical teachings of the Torah, it is taught that pride and haughtiness are generally an anathema to maintaining a spiritual relationship with God, or even a physical relationship for that matter, as misplaced pride gets in the way.

However, to be proud of one's heritage, Jewishness, connection to the Divine or one's commitment to moral values, is perfectly appropriate pride and is highly encouraged.

YOM KIPPUR – OUT OF THE BOX THINKING

So, Rosh Hashana has passed, and we are getting ready for Yom Kippur. We did our part by entreating God for a good year, and we are confident that God will grant our request in abundance.

Let's talk Yom Kippur.

The holiday of Yom Kippur, when you think about it, is a tremendous gift. All we have to do is fast for 25 hours, ask for forgiveness for our transgressions, wrongdoings and misbehavior, and voila, we have a completely new slate. It is like the sins never happened.

The key ingredients needed are as follows - sincerity, humility and awareness. The Yom Kippur prayer book gives us the outline of how to confess silently and directly to God about the various behaviors that are abhorrent in God's eyes. Essentially, we make an accounting of what we did wrong and then we regret what we did and then, most importantly, we resolve to make every effort to not repeat the same mistakes.

Most important to point out is, for interpersonal wrongdoings, atoning before God is of no consequence and we must address the person whom we have hurt, maligned or cheated. The Code of Jewish Law states clearly "God is unable to forgive interpersonal grievances, and that these have to be directed to the offended individuals."

There is another element of Yom Kippur which is so out of the box, most people are not even aware that it even exists. Rav Kook, who was the first Ashkenazi Chief Rabbi of Palestine in 1921, wrote that in order to have a true and proper spiritual accounting of our Souls, we must also include the good we have done and not just the bad.

The following is the text of the short confessional that we recite 10 times throughout Yom Kippur.

We have trespassed;

We have dealt treacherously;

We have robbed;

We have spoken slander;

We have acted perversely;

We have done wrong;

We have acted presumptuously;

We have done violence;

We have practiced deceit;

We have counseled evil;

We have spoken falsehood;

We have scoffed;

We have revolted;

We have blasphemed;

We have rebelled;

We have committed iniquity;

We have transgressed;

We have oppressed;

We have been stiff necked;

We have acted wickedly;

We have dealt corruptly;

We have committed abominations;

We have gone astray;

We have led others astray.

In addition to the above, Rav Kook suggests that we also say the following.

We have loved;

We have blessed;

We have grown;

We have spoken positively;

We have raised up;

We have shown compassion;

We have acted enthusiastically;

We have been empathetic;

We have cultivated truth;

We have given good advice;

We have respected;

We have learned;

We have forgiven;

We have comforted;

We have been creative;

We have stirred;

We have been spiritual activists,

We have been just;

We have longed for Moshiach/Messiah;

We have been merciful;

We have given full effort;

We have supported;

We have contributed;

We have repaired.

Go ahead and confess, but always remember to recognize the good you have done. God needs to hear you say that you love yourself and so do you.

With blessings for a meaningful Yom Kippur and an easy fast.

KABBALISTIC INSIGHTS

Self-worth is a building block of our life. It is what allows us to be whom we are. Without self-worth, we would never be able to master a job interview or compete in sports, etc.

Interesting to note. Children have an abundance of self-worth. It is only through life's challenges that we can lose it. I once heard that the reason as to why adults are called adults, it is because they get "adulterated."

THE CORONAVIRUS AND PURIM

A KABBALISTIC PARADOX

Unless you live in a different universe, all you hear on planet earth is talk of the Coronavirus, also known as Covid-19. The discussions revolve around how many people are affected or quarantined in your state, county or city; which schools are closed; and where does one purchase toilet paper or hand sanitizer in bulk.

In my entire recollection of events, I cannot remember being so information overloaded. We live in a time of modern communication – we know exactly how many people in China are sick, with which virus and what particular strain. I do not recall hearing anything of Corona 1 through 18, have you? The constant overabundance of reporting is leading to mass hysteria. We are petrified that we are going to get quarantined or worse sick and die. This is causing us to fall apart and fist fight over toilet paper.

As a Rabbi, I am constantly asked my thoughts about many things and the Coronavirus is no exception. What are we to make of all this? What should be my response as a Jewish (hopefully spiritual) leader of a diverse community?

I have given this much thought and I have concluded that it is no accident that the Jewish holiday of Purim, has certain similarities to a dreaded epidemic.

In the story of Purim, we read how the enemies of the Jews had conspired to kill anyone of the Jewish faith in one single day. The killing was to be completely indiscriminatory, other than being Jews; be it man, woman or child or even Jewish babies. The killers were granted in advance full immunity from the crown. This was state sanctioned murder at its best. There was no escape as the crown ruled 127 provinces and the Jews had nowhere to flee from this cruel edict.

It is fascinating to read in the Purim story what the Jewish response was. I believe we can learn a thing or two from the story of Purim as it pertains to our current situation.

LESSON #1 - STRATEGIC

One of the ways that the Jewish leadership of the Purim story dealt with this horrific pending pandemic of Jew hatred was to go to the crown directly and appeal for repeal of the dastardly decree. They knew that in addition to praying for miracles they had to deal with the establishment as well. They recognized the need to tackle this organically, as well as spiritually.

We can learn from this that while we need to hope and pray for miracles, we also need to live in this world. We need to practice reasonable caution to protect ourselves from possible contamination. This would include avoiding locations that were exposed and following instructions like not touching your face, washing hands and limiting personal contact to fist bumps, etc.

LESSON #2 – SPIRITUAL

The hero and heroine of the story of Purim understood that they did not only live in one dimension strictly governed by physicality and nature. They understood that life and death, sickness and health are in the hands of God. If God decrees that a person die, for whatever reason, then this is the Divine will and there is very little that can be done. Conversely, if God wills a person to recover, even if doctors say otherwise, God will prevail. There is a fellow in our community whose father was stricken with cancer and given a few months to live. Well, his father beat the odds and survived another 20 years! It was simply not his time. Mordechai & Esther, the two forces of good in the times of the Purim story, gathered together 22,000 children in prayer. They recognized that while strategy and diplomacy were vastly important, it needs to compiled with entreaty and petition to the "Great One."

We too need to understand and appreciate this concept of spirituality. We need to beg, implore, beseech and storm the heavens in prayer asking God to assuage our pain, fears and suffering. Prayer for help is not just relegated to the Jewish High Holidays. Reaching out to a power beyond us is not only a gift from above, it is also our obligation. Simply stated, we need to pray time and time again.

LESSON #3 – JOY

Lastly, Judaism stresses that we must be joyous even in the face of adversity. There is a line toward the end of the Megillah which states that the Jewish people had "sasson and simcha," which are different types of joy. There is bliss that we feel at a wedding called simcha, and then there is a joy called sasson, which does not hinge upon anything in particular.

We need not walk around all worried and anxious as to when the other shoe filled with Coronavirus will drop on our lap. We need to be prudent and joyous at the same time. My parents were fond of saying, "If I cry for nothing, then they will give me something to cry about." I believe that most were brought up this way as well. The Kabbalah and the Megillah teach us that we need to revise this colloquial parental statement to, "If you are happy for nothing (sasson), then I will give you something to be happy about."

KABBALISTIC INSIGHTS

The entire story of Purim was one of many miracles coming together to save the Jews. The miracles were not apparent like the splitting of the sea or the daily manna from heaven. The Purim miracles were enclothed in nature. We are taught that a bona fide miracle albeit hidden in nature, where it takes effort to analyze is much loftier than an apparent miracle.

THE KABBALAH OF THE 10 PLAGUES

HOW TO AVOID IRRITANTS & AGGRAVATION

One of the fundamentals of Judaism is to recount the biblical story of the exodus from Egypt. You see, every facet of the exodus can have deep meaning in our lives, and the 10 plagues of affliction is no exception.

During the plagues, the Pharaoh and his countrymen were taught several lessons for their crimes against humanity. The Kabbalah teaches us that each of the plagues is a life lesson for us, even living thousands of years later.

The following are some of the teachings of the practical application of the plagues: How to know when we are being plagued or what to think about when things do not seem to be working out.

I am happy to present a synopsis. I hope you enjoy this as much as I did. Some are originally mine.

BLOOD

The practical lesson here, says the Kabbalah, is that the temperature of water is cold, which is synonymous with a lack of passion in life, while the temp of blood is warm, which indicates passion. One of the first plagues that afflicts human beings is apathy and a lack of caring. This needs to be corrected. One needs to develop a passion and a zest for life. Apathy and indifference are the first ingredients of a slippery slope to a meaningless life.

FROGS

Another thing to consider is how much extraneous noise we have in our life. How much stimulation do we really need to survive? Are we bogged down by possessions that make our lives harder instead of easier? Do we have "friends" who are really "frenemies?" We need to constantly assess whether the things we own or the people we choose to hang out with are positive or causing us to croak?

LICE

The little things that needle us constantly need to be eliminated otherwise they become constant irritants. The lice plague teaches us that when we have too many things that bother us, it becomes a great distraction and causes us to be dysfunctional. I stopped buying newspapers or going on to select news sites because I found that the bias was making me upset. We need to purge the annoying stuff and focus more on what is healing and therapeutic.

WILD BEASTS

The Yiddish word for wild beasts is "vilde chayas." Colloquially speaking, it means children who are out of control due to being spoiled and pampered, who have no obligations or responsibilities required of them. Rearing an indulged child is an epic mistake, as this child will grow to be a wild ass of a human with no regard for his/her fellow person. He/she will expect to gain but never to give. Be forewarned.

PESTILENCE

Shakespeare's definition is almost prophetic. He writes "I will pour pestilence in his ear." Pestilence is any destructive power. It could be the bubonic or black plague or it could be as unassuming as gossip. You must understand that slander, gossip, insult, defamation are all levels of pestilence that can make many people sick. Stay away from the rumormongers or talebearers as they can be just as deadly spiritually to one's soul as a coronavirus is to the body.

BOILS

Boils are a euphemism for many things that can cause you to blow your top, cause the skin on your face to turn red in fury and make your blood boil. Anything that gets you angry has to be addressed immediately. Anger is considered to be one of the biggest negatives in our lives. It is so egregious to lose one's temper that the Talmud equates it to idol worship. In short, anger is a plague that needs to be curbed as soon as possible as there is no redeeming quality to uncontrolled anger.

HAIL OF FIRE & ICE

During this unique plague, God united fire and ice to mix together to cause maximum destruction on the Egyptians. The lesson of this most unusual mix is that we too need to seek compromise as often as we can, as we, like the hail, are messengers of the Almighty. If we can only see one side of the argument than we are by definition, limited. However, if we push ourselves to go beyond our comfort zone, and see a perspective from someone else's point of view, then we become Godly.

LOCUSTS

Locusts swarm in huge numbers, consume the produce and create chaos. Disorganization, disorder and inefficiency is chaotic and will literally destroy productivity. Living one's life in confusion with no clarity or direction is toxic for the body and soul and will lead to complete deer in the headlights type of existence, where one does not know which way to turn. To be organized in one's mind takes hard work, but it will lessen the swarm of voices in one's brain and will lead to great potentials.

DARKNESS

Depression is all dark all the time. In discussing this plague, the Torah relates that there were two levels of darkness. One that no one could see through and the other so thick that even movement was not possible. Depression is just like that. It begins with a dark outlook and then it locks one up to the point that one cannot get out of bed. Depression is a plague that must be countered and met head on, whether a medical professional in the case of a clinical depression or a clergy member for advice on how to lead a meaningful life. Do not ever let darkness overcome you. Try to live in the light.

DEATH OF THE FIRSTBORN

We see that Pharaoh was only moved to act and allow the Hebrews to leave Egypt when it got real up close and personal. Until the point where he was personally affected, he remained aloof and unmoved. It took his son's death to make him open his heart to allow these beaten people to leave his country of horrors. We need to be involved personally in our community and not just a voyeur. We need to be immersed in a very deep way in our kid's academic and social lives. We should not be the type of people who turn a blind eye and a deaf ear to those less fortunate, but rather we should be involved and passionately moved to make positive changes where and whenever we can.

KABBALISTIC INSIGHTS

A deeper teaching into the 10 plagues. They were essentially a war strategy. First Moses and Aaron came to Pharaoh with a just request of let the slaves go. When Pharaoh did not heed the 10 plagues were thrust upon them.

Economic damage: Plagues of blood, death of livestock, hail, and locusts.

Physical damage: Plagues of frogs, lice, wild animals, and boils.

Demoralizing the enemy: Plague of Darkness and death of the firstborn.

RECIPROCITY – A PASSOVER MUSING

JUDAISM'S UNIQUE TAKE ON APPRECIATION

One of my favorite lessons that I have learned comes from a unique perspective mentioned in the Torah. This teaching really resonates with me and should be, in my opinion, taught in schools, despite the separation of church and state.

A different portion of the Torah/Bible is read each week publicly in the synagogue on Shabbat/Saturday morning. The Torah is most definitely not a history book, but rather, it is a book of incredible teachings, morals, values and lessons. Interesting to note: there are parts of the Torah that are not even written in chronological order!! Because it is not a history book.

One of the Torah portions discusses in great lengths the Ten Plagues that befell the Egyptians for enslaving the ancient Hebrews (my great granddaddy) and for defying the call to let them go free.

The Torah tells us that the first few plagues were not administered directly by Moses, but by the hand of his brother Aharon. The next few plagues, however, were administered by Moses himself. The reason for the change in administration is such a beautiful lesson.

Moses could not be involved in the first two because they involved water. The first plague was that the water was turned to blood and the second plague was the emergence of hundreds of thousands of frogs from the River Nile.

Parenthetically, I remember one-night walking around the lodge in the bush of Krueger Park, South Africa, and suddenly I saw a huge frog emerge from the trees and I was literally frozen in my tracks, traumatized. Interestingly enough, psychologists call it "ranidaphobia."

Back to the present. The reason why Moses could not be involved with polluting the water was because it was water that saved Moses from drowning EIGHTY YEARS before. As you may know, when baby Moses was born, he was placed in a basket and hidden in the bulrushes as King Pharaoh had decreed that all Hebrew boys should be killed. There was no way Moses could in any way "hurt" the water as this very same River Nile was the very same entity that "helped" him. Therefore, the task was handed to someone else.

Think about this for a moment. While it is true that water is a living element, it nonetheless does not have any feeling, and will not get insulted or embarrassed if you turn your back on it. Yet, Moses could not bring himself to smite or contaminate the water because it did him a favor. WHEN? 80 years ago! Moses did not adopt the attitude of what have you done for me lately. Moses could not and would not turn his back on something that was kind to him.

What a lesson!!

How much more does this lesson apply with a fellow human being with feelings and emotions? Don't let the fact that you don't really have anything to do with a person anymore interfere with how you reciprocate. If one is given the chance to return a kindness, even many years later, you should go ahead and seize the opportunity.

Perhaps this is why in the laws of a Jewish burial everyone is afforded the opportunity to pick up a shovel and put earth over the casket. We do not just leave it to the professionals. You see, this is the last occasion to physically reciprocate a kindness to someone who shared a caring word with you. However, do not wait until they die. Reciprocity is more powerful when they are alive.

KABBALISTIC INSIGHTS

In one of the earlier Mishnah it reads,

Whoever does not need to take [gifts for the poor] but takes, will not die of old age until he becomes dependent on people. And whoever needs to take but does not take will not die of old age until he supports others from his own. And similarly, a judge who renders a true judgement according to its truth. And anyone who is neither lame, nor blind, nor crippled, but makes himself as one who is, will not die of old age until he becomes like one of them.

I call this Jewish Karma.

SHAVUOT: JEWISH LAW & HEALTH

In a few days, Jewish people around the world will be celebrating the Biblical holiday of Shavout. This most important holiday commemorates the giving of the Torah to the Israelites 50 days after their release from Egyptian bondage.

Most years there is a galvanizing of the troops. All Jewish men, women and children are encouraged to come to the Synagogue and hear the 10 Commandments (not suggestions) being read publicly. The purpose of this effort is not only to hear the Commandments being read, but also to reaffirm the bond that was made when the Torah was originally given.

However, this year is not like most years. This year we are living through an unprecedented time of a pandemic – a global virus that attacks indiscriminately. We have therefore been placed in quarantine and isolation in order to stem the virus' vicious attacks, and of course flatten the curve. This year, most Jewish establishments will be closed, and even if open, will be limited to only 10 people (except scofflaws).

So, how does this reconcile with the reaffirmation of the bond if we cannot get to the services to hear the 10 Commandments being read? Most people are nervous to venture out even if allowed. Does this mean that our bond is diminished? Are we "bad' if we do not hear? Are we less devout or connected?

The following response may or may not surprise you. There is a Jewish law that in order to save a life, especially one's own life, one is allowed to not only be excused from normative Jewish behavior and expectations, but even more so, one is allowed to transgress a Biblical command. Furthermore, it is not only ok to transgress a law, it is encouraged. A sick person (not minor colds guys) must eat and drink on Yom Kippur if we even remotely suspect that this person's very life is in danger. Furthermore, if the possibly dangerously sick person refuses, we coerce him/her to eat as saving a life is a Mitzvah in itself.

The rationale is that we were created to be humans in physical bodies with souls. The purpose of our coming down to earth is to do as many of the Commandments/good deeds as possible during our lifetime. If we therefore consciously allow our lives to be shortened as in the above example of not eating on Yom Kippur, it is not considered a noble act of martyrdom, but rather a foolish one. Consequently, logic follows. If the above-mentioned person does in fact eat on Yom Kippur, he should do so without guilt knowing that he/she is doing a Mitzvah and gets to live another day.

Going back to Shavuot. These are not normal times and there is definitely sufficient cause to be nervous of one's health. Things do seem to be getting better but we are for the most part not there yet.

Therefore, if one is nervous to venture out to hear the 10 Commandments because of health considerations, then not only should there be no guilt or remorse, one should also be happy that they are doing a Mitzvah.

And here is the point. The best way to strengthen the bond with God is by fulfilling His wishes, and if by staying home you are saving a life, then realize that you are doing what God wants you to do and this is a Mitzvah.

Having said the above, as of writing this the Governor of New York State does allow for services to be held with severe restrictions. Therefore, if you feel healthy and are willing to abide by ALL the rules, then maybe you can go. I say this because there are people who will go because it is important to them and they should NOT be frowned upon or judged. Each individual person should decide for themselves and then live and let live as there is no right or wrong.

In the interim enjoy the solitude – you are doing a Mitzvah.

KABBALISTIC INSIGHTS

The ancient Midrash relates, God agreed to give the Torah to the Jewish people only after the children were offered as "guarantors," ensuring that the Torah would be learned, cherished and observed for generations to come.

The Lubavitcher Rebbe—Rabbi Menachem M. Schneerson, of righteous memory—called upon every Jewish man woman and child, even babies to be present in the synagogue on the morning of the first day of Shavuot, when the Ten Commandments are read as part of continuing the "guarantee" that was made over 3300 years ago.

A JEWISH THOUGHT ON THANKSGIVING

We are about to celebrate the Thanksgiving holiday filled with joy and thanks for family and friends.

Interesting to note that the term "Jew" and the term "thanks" are actually synonymous.

You see the Torah records that Jacob had 12 sons, which became the foundation for the 12 tribes of Israel. One would think that we should be called Jacobis after Jacob, or Reubens (we do have the most delicious sandwich named after him though), or Reubs after the firstborn son of Israel. Instead, we are called Yehudim, named after the fourth son of Jacob who was called Yehuda, which in English transliteration is Judah, in German/Yiddish is Jud/Yud and in America (and other places) Jew.

Why pick this name and not any other?

The Torah gives the reasons as to why Jacob and his wives (mainly the mothers named the children) named each one the way they did.

Reuvain comes from two words Re'u Vain. See I have a son. Leah, his mother, felt vindicated that she had given Jacob his firstborn.

Shimon is comprised also of two words. Shim On. Heard my suffering. Leah felt that God has heard her prayers.

Levi means accompaniment. Leah now knew that Jacob will have to accompany her on trips to the well as they have three kids and she only has two hands.

Now we come to Yehuda. Leah called him so because she wished to thank God for giving her a fourth son. There were four wives and there were destined to be 12 children. Leah was thankful that she had her fair share of the 12 tribes.

This is a great lesson.

We are called Jew and not Rubies because this is our essence. We need to be thankful. We need to criticize less and thank more. We need to acknowledge someone's kindness to us and not take them for granted. We need to be thankful to God for our lives, our parents for rearing us, and our teachers for educating us. And on and on and on.

Another fascinating Jewish tidbit: We are taught that we are upon awakening each morning to recite a short prayer BEFORE getting out of bed. The prayer is called Modeh Ani. It literally gives thanks to God for giving us yet another day to fulfill our particular mission here on earth.

This prayer is not just recited on one's birthday or a day dedicated to thanks, but rather every single day. Day in and day out, we say Modeh Ani – our thanks - and we do so as soon as we open our eyes.

An important point to consider though: Don't wait until Thanksgiving to thank someone. Offer your thanks immediately. I always cite the following example. If a neighbor drops off a bag of rock salt as a favor, do not wait until you see him/her in the diner, store or nail place. Call them up immediately, before the sun sets and offer your sincerest appreciation.

Thank you to the USA for absorbing me and my wife into this country. I hope we have made you just as proud as we are of you.

I would like to share a Jewish prayer found in a book called "The Secrets and Roots to Our Work," written by Rabbi Alexander Diskin around 200 years ago.

Thank You Hashem (God), King of Kings and Master of the World!

Thank You for the infinite times that You helped me, supported me, rescued me, encouraged me, cured me, guarded over me and made me happy.

Thank You for always being with me.

Thank You for giving me the strength to observe Your commandments, to do good deeds and pray. Thank You for all the times You helped me and I didn't know how to say "Thank You."

Thank You for all the loving kindnesses You do for me each and every moment. Thank You for every breath I breathe.

Thank You, Hashem, for all the things that I do have, and thank You, Hashem, even for the things that I don't have.

Thank You for my periodic difficulties, my occasional setbacks, and for the times when I don't feel happy, because everything is for my ultimate benefit, even if I don't see that it's always for my best...

Deep in my heart, I know that everything that comes from You is the very best for me and designed especially for me in precision and exacting Divine Providence, of which only The King of Kings is capable.

Thank You for the periodic times that are difficult for me, for only that way they enable me to fully appreciate the good times, for only after being in darkness one can appreciate the light.

Thank You for the wonderful life You have given me.

Thank You for every little thing that I have, for everything comes from You and from no one else.

Thank You for always listening to my prayers.

Creator of the World, I apologize from the bottom of my heart for all the times that I didn't appreciate what You gave me, and instead of thanking You I only complained.

I am dust and ashes and You are the entire universe. Please, don't ever cast me away.

KABBALSITIC INSIGHTS

There are a few places in the Midrash where it discusses that when the Messiah comes and we enter into the Messianic period, all communal animal sacrifices will cease except the todah/thanksgiving one.

This lesson is most powerful. The redemption may bring many changes into our lives but the one constant is the need to always be thankful.

Saying or doing one's thanks is one of the things that make us human.

THOUGHTS ON LIFE

KABBALAH OF CONTEMPORARY IDOLS

BE CAREFUL OF THESE TWO PITFALLS

According to the biblical history of Judea, idol worship ceased after the destruction of the First Temple. In the Book of Kings, which discusses the various kings and queens who reigned over Israel, it teaches about the unthinkable multitudes of idols and idol worshippers who existed among the Jewish people.

One example would be the wicked usurper queen Ataliah, who brought Ba'al worship to Jerusalem. Ahaz, father of Hezekiah, built an altar in the Temple, and his grandson Menasseh worshiped both the idols Ba'al and Astarte there.

What is fascinating is that after the destruction of the First Temple, we hear no more of idolatry. Those who were exiled during the destruction went to Babylon and were instructed by Jeremiah to accept their fate, settle down and rebuild their lives. True, there was some attempt to force idol worship during the second Temple period, but it was quickly squashed by the Maccabees, the heroes of the Chanukah story who cleansed the Temple and stopped any form of idol worship.

However, is it true that idol worship has died out? Furthermore, is it true today?

CLASSICAL MONEY WORSHIP

What is interesting to note is there is an actual disorder called "money worship." In Psychology Today there are a slew of articles that deal with this disorder. It pretty much sums money worship up like this: stockpiling objects or money provides a sense of safety, security, and relief of anxiety. "Compulsive buying" is overspending on steroids. Compulsive shoppers are consumed by their money worries. These patterns are usually self-destructive. Additionally, they can easily put a limit on who you are as a person as well as your financial success.

KABBALISTIC MONEY IDOL

I wish to address money as an idol in the Kabbalistic sense, which does not necessarily preclude the above, but rather fleshes it out more in a definitive Jewish way.

There is a classic Jewish metaphor on the difference between a plain piece of glass, a windowpane where one can look out onto the street and gaze at people, cars and squirrels, and a mirror where one can only see their reflection. They are both made of glass and are in fact still simple plates of glass, except one has a shiny metallic silvery adhesive which turns it into a mirror. All it takes, explains the sages, is an extremely thin piece of silver to change one's perspective from seeing others to only seeing oneself.

If making and retaining money makes one callous to someone else's plight, or if upward mobility from a bad neighborhood to a beautiful one makes one feel better than you and one looks down on others who still live in the hood, then this is what we also call money worship. After all what has changed?

There is no coincidence that on the dollar bill it has these epic words "In God We Trust." I think the previous generations understood the risks of money and how it can turn a giving person into a stingy one, an inherently selfless person into a selfish one. So, they imprinted it onto each and every piece of negotiable tender available at that time.

It is vital that we check and recheck ourselves to make sure that money does not change us and that we are not worshipping a contemporary idol.

EGO – THE WORSHIP OF SELF.

I do not remember who shared with me that the word EGO is an acronym for Easing God Out. I believe that it is a brilliant concept. You see, when a person only cares about themselves and no one else, then aside from being selfish, this hapless individual can be termed a self-worshipper.

To clarify some more….

An egomaniac is a person who is obsessively egotistical or self-centered. They have no time for you or God. They only have time to further their own goals, which is perceived as the most important thing they can do.

This is not to negate that every person has to have a healthy sense of self, just that it cannot only be about yourself. As the Lubavitcher Rebbe once wrote

Say, "I need to make this happen."

Say, "I have to see this done."

Not only is this "I" permissible, it is crucial to your mission in life.

So, when does ego become evil?

When it believes the "I" is your mission in life.

BOTTOM LINE

Be careful of being so self-absorbed that you will not hear the cry of another. We were brought to this earth to not only take care of ourselves and our immediate family, we were created to make a major difference in the world and this means being ready to help, assist and support those who cross our paths.

KABBALSITIC INSIGHTS

Truth be told, there is another common form of idol worship today in addition to the aforementioned, and this would be the general idea of idol worship, in essence ignoring God. When we put our complete reliance on the Government or another human without placing our Creator in the midst, this would be construed as idolatry. Unfortunately, this is a tale as old as time.

KABBALISTIC INSIGHTS – FREE WILL

PERCEPTIONS THAT CAN CHANGE YOUR LIFE

As part of my daily regimen, I try to fulfill my quota of reading and studying. One of the books that I read/study daily is the Tanya, which was written in 1795. It is a book that has changed my life as it has enhanced my understanding of life and has given me insights that I would never have gleaned if not for this book. Over the course of the next few columns, I hope to capture some amazing life lessons learned.

HAPPENSTANCE/RANDOMNESS

The Tanya teaches that everything we encounter, observe, perceive or witness is pre-ordained and not happenstance, random or left to chance. The fact that two strangers meet is because it is supposed to happen. I take my life as an example. I was born in London, England, and my parents immigrated to New York City when I was a teenager. My wife was born in South Africa and her parents immigrated to California when she was a pre-teen. We met in Brooklyn when my wife was studying here. Our respective footsteps were guided and now we have our own dynasty. My mentor once told me that when two unfamiliar persons meet, the goal is that it should benefit an unrelated third person.

Likewise, when a person passes from this world, it is not a random act, but rather part of a master plan. We do not know why someone passes at 79, 89, 99 or 59. We are taught that only God has the "keys" to the book of life. However, what we do know (and this is why when someone passes, we recite the Kaddish prayer) is that it had nothing to do with random luck, fortune or a fluke or even good genes. Rather, all is preordained. As we will see below, that yes, it is possible to tempt fate.

A most fundamental question that comes immediately to mind is the following. If everything is pre-ordained then why bother doing anything at all? If it is meant to be then it is meant to be?

There are a couple of answers that resonate with me and I will attempt to convey them to the best of my ability.

1. The first answer to this most complex question is that regardless of free will, we still need to create a vessel, a receptacle for the blessings and for

what is meant to be. Take the marriage example above. If we refuse to date anyone, then chances are we will never meet someone special in life to marry. Another example, if you never purchase a lottery ticket then you will never win the jackpot even if you were supposed to. Or, if one feels chest pain and chooses to ignore it instead of being checked out to "possibly" prolong life, then this is called not properly creating or preparing the vessel for blessings. Likewise, with the other two examples, we are not creating the vessels for God's blessings.

2. Another interesting take is that free will is only in moral decisions. Whether one likes chocolate or vanilla ice cream, this is not true free will, but rather a pre-programmed chip. I do not like cottage cheese and believe me this has nothing to do with my free will. What is moral is a hotly contested issue and will be addressed perhaps at another time, but suffice it to say it is not whether we prefer white gold to yellow or rose gold.

KABBALASTIC INSIGHTS

When we are at a delta, a moral crossroads, and we need to decide to choose this moral path or the other path which is not morally acceptable. We should know and realize that despite the fact that God knows our end game and our decisions way ahead of us. His knowledge however, will have no bearing and not affect our decision-making process in the moment. Choose wisely.

LIVE IN THE PRESENT NO REGRETS

There is a fascinating verse in the beginning of Torah that brings up so many questions: "And the Lord repented that He had made man on the earth, and it grieved Him in His heart. And the Lord said, 'I will destroy man whom I have created from the face of the earth, both man and beast, and the creeping thing and the fowls of the air, for I repent that I have made them.'"

How could that be when He knows the end before the beginning?

The great commentator Rashi discusses a possible explanation: A heretic asked R. Joshua ben Korchah: "Don't you Jews say that G d knows the future?"

Rabbi Joshua answered, "Yes."

"Why then," continued the heretic, "is it written that it 'grieved Him in His heart?'"

Responded R. Joshua, "Was a son ever born to you?"

"Yes," said the heretic.

"What did you do?"

"I rejoiced."

"But didn't you know that one day he will die?"

Replied the man, "One rejoices when it is a time for rejoicing, and one mourns when it is a time for mourning."

Said R. Joshua, "So it is with God."

Rashi, adds a few words to explain further. He adds, "Although it was known to Him that they will sin and be destroyed, He nevertheless created them for the sake of the righteous who will descend from them." Meaning that G d created humankind because He wanted righteous human beings. So, when He created them, He rejoiced. He knew there would be wicked people, for there cannot be righteousness without wickedness, good without bad. But now was a time to rejoice. Later, when the wicked would arise, that would be the time to mourn.

I believe that there are many lessons to be learned from the above dialogue. However, for space sake I wish to focus on just two.

FAMILY PLANNING

I believe the first lesson is that while planning ahead is important, it should never distract us from our ultimate purpose. As an example, I have met many people who do not "plan" to have children because they are not sure if they will be able to handle kids, whether emotionally, financially or physically. Well, to be honest when I had my first child at 24, I too did not know whether I could either handle children for the aforementioned reasons, but I refused to let it distract me from my higher purpose of bringing children into the world. When I am asked if I believe in family planning, my response is always "I planned to have a family." In my opinion, everyone needs to plan to have a family, but if life or God dictates otherwise, then I get it. We however, must not over plan our lives to our complete detriment.

The above is just one example where we over plan, and instead of making life better, it actually ruins us. Another example would be money. Too many people are fixated on dollars and cents so much so that they actually lose their morals and sense. I know a man who earns a fantastic living but is so paranoid about not/never having enough that he will not allow the family to go out to eat even on special occasions. There are no family vacations, no birthday or graduation presents, etc. I know this is an extreme case but how many of us can relate to this idea that money is so controlling that it leads to mental ruination and complete life control as opposed to us being in charge of our money.

Even the best-laid plans are thwarted and need adjusting. Therefore, when our plans get upset, we need to adjust and live in the moment and not get bogged down or allow ourselves to get destroyed by too much planning. Be a little flexible and very satisfied with your lot.

SAVE THE WORLD

The second lesson is that while God knew that there would be bad people, He still created and saved the world because of the good people. The lesson is obvious — be a saver and not a destroyer. Practically this means as follows, when one is at a delta and is confronted by a moral dilemma, we have at that moment of time a choice to make. We have the ability to bring ourselves down into the moral abyss or reach new heights of morality.

Up to us and no one else. Good luck and may the force be with you.

KABBALISTIC INSIGHTS

In our daily prayers we recite that each and every day God renews the world. This teaches us that we need to live in the present and not in the past nor the future. As the Talmud says, "The past is the past and who knows what the future holds, and the present is like a blink of an eye. So, why worry.

CAN MIRACLES HAPPEN TODAY?

We are in the midst of Chanukah, a Jewish festive holiday in which we commemorate not one, but two awesome miracles.

The first miracle was the fact that a small band of heroic men beat back a massive army of Greek soldiers. If wagers were to be held in Vegas, the Greeks would have been a sure victory if not for a miracle that occurred that the Greeks gave up prematurely.

The second miracle was that the Israelites only found one jug of pure olive oil with the seal of the high priest still intact. The oil was only enough to last one night, but miraculously lasted for 8 nights until the Israelites could secure more pure oil.

So, the obvious question that comes to mind is, do miracles happen today? And I believe that the answer is that they absolutely do.

You see sometimes we witness a miracle but we either are so clouded by cynicism or believe a natural explanation given for unnatural facts, that we end up dismissing what is an actual, bona fide miracle as nothing special.

THE SIX DAY WAR

Take for example the following story, which is in fact, a miracle similar to the first aforementioned miracle of Chanukah. This happened in 1967 during the Six Day War.

According to all the military analysts, Israel was going to lose and lose badly. The Israel Defense Forces (IDF) consisted of 275,000 troops, compared to the 456,000 soldiers of the combined Iraqi, Syrian, Jordanian and Egyptian armies. The united Arab forces also had much more military equipment at their disposal. The Arab forces had more than double the number of tanks, and close to four times the amount of combat aircraft. The Israeli civilians and military were filled with dread, shock and fright for the upcoming battle.

So pessimistic was the outlook that the nation's national parks were marked to become gravesites for the many who would perish in the course of the war.

However, despite all the predictions, by the time the war ended, the territory under Israeli control had tripled in size. Jews returned to sites where their ancestors had lived for thousands of years, sites from which waves of terror were launched against them for so many years. One of the craziest stories happened on the sixth and final day of the war, where not unlike the Greeks in the Chanukah story, the 75,000 strong Syrian army simply fled from the mountains of the Golan Heights leaving their weaponry behind. The strategic Golan upon which the Syrians used to murder Israelis were now in the hands of the Israeli army.

SAADAM HUSSEIN AND 39 SCUDS

The miracles experienced in Israel during the Gulf War are too numerous to mention. The television was filled with images of people buried in rubble, yet walking away without a scratch. In all, 39 scud missiles fell – many in heavily populated areas – causing only two deaths. Can you imagine 39 missiles and only two deaths? Altogether over ten tons of explosives fell on Israel; 15,000 properties were damaged which included 10,992 apartments, 235 houses and 3773 other buildings.

In all 13 people died. Two directly from a missile and 11 indirectly from heart attacks or misuse of a gasmask. Scuds landed between two buildings but did not explode and the list goes on and on. A true miracle.

But Rabbi, do miracles happen today?

YES!!!

I believe that conception is a miracle and that birth is miraculous. I also believe that the sun rising in the east and setting in the west each and every day is a miracle. The fact that there is enough of an atmosphere to sustain this planet as opposed to other planets is supernatural.

Furthermore, I am the first to state that The Chai Center, the organization that I founded, is a miracle. I continue to see miracles and have angelic encounters with beautiful people who share my vision.

KABBALISTIC INSIGHTS

In a very famous letter by Rabbi Solomon Shlumil of Dreznitz in 1607, to his relatives in Bohemia after immigrating to Safed in 1602. He writes about the "wondrous things that the great Kabbalist, Rabbi Isaac Luria originally of Jerusalem, miracles that have not been seen in the entire land since the days of the tanna'im. (220 C.E.)."

In the letter Shlumil clarifies the miracles "He had knowledge of the wisdom that was in the countenance and soul of human beings and their incarnations and could say what evil men had been reincarnated in trees, stones, or in beasts and fowl, and he could say what transgressions a man had made from the commandments and the transgressions [he had committed] since his childhood, and he had knowledge of when amends had been made for this fault, and he had knowledge of the chirping of the birds, etc."

THE LEVELS OF LIVING

PLEASURE vs. PAIN

I was asked a question the other day and I answered with what I thought was the most obvious response. The question posited was – What is the opposite of pain? I responded, pleasure. What would you have said?

The questioner responded that he believes that I am incorrect and that the correct answer is "NO pain." While this is something more for Confucius than yours truly, it got me on a track of thought that I believe is worth writing about.

Bear with me.

There are many ways to go through life, and yes, some are more fortunate than others. It is true that there are some who everything seems to go their way in terms of looks, money, fame and luck. And yes, it is also true that there are others whose lives seem to be lacking in many areas, and where nothing seems to be going right. The reality is, however, and this is a crucial truism: There are five big words that we should repeat as our mantra, "WE ARE NOT IN CONTROL." There are so many things in life, whether pain or pleasure, that we can absolutely do nothing about. As an example, we cannot change how tall we are (this Rabbi knows that elevator shoes are not worth the money). The only thing we can do is change how we feel about it and decide if this particular issue is going to be very painful to us or not. Is what happened going to destroy us or can we rise out of the ashes like a phoenix stronger than we were before? Much of life's challenges are more about how we react to the challenge than the test itself. Viktor Frankl says it best in his book, "Man in Search of Meaning."

Let me give you an example to hopefully illustrate the point.

There are three ways to fly. There is first class, which is magnificent. You are living it up luxuriously. You get to Europe refreshed, full and ready to take on the day. Parenthetically, be careful, once you fly like this there is no going back. Then there is business class. This is also an unbelievable experience. While not as pampered as the upper class, it is still an incredible way to fly. The next level of flight is economy. The airlines do not wish to call it third class so they wised up and call it economy to applaud you for being more frugal with your money. Now economy is a more difficult flight, crammed like sardines with no legroom, but it is still way better than the next level, which is flying with the animals and baggage. There are no amenities in the baggage hold and definitely no peanuts or inflight TV.

Now let's take two different people from very different backgrounds. On the one hand, there is someone like Derek Jeter. If you stuck him in economy class, he would probably back out of the journey and let you know that you will be hearing from his team of lawyers and he is done flying commercial.

However, what if you take a Sudanese boy, Srinwantu Dey, and fly him out of his war-torn country. He could care less which class of service he is in. In fact, he would settle for an oxygen mask and a piece of rope tied to the outside of the plane because he is focused on the goal of surviving to live another day. He is not bogged down by the lack of ambience, etc.

It is really up to us. Are we going to let our day-to-day issues ruin our lives and live-in immense pain? Or are we going to be thankful for our life and try and squeeze out a little pleasure?

It is way easier to be cynical, bitter and see the cup half empty than to be happy and positive. This is why in Judaism there is a Mitzvah, which loosely translates as an obligation to be happy. We need to be commanded to be happy because it is sometimes very tough.

The message is clear.

1. Don't get bogged down by the small stuff and instead choose to be happy.

2. Please realize that attitude is 95% of living.

3. Lastly, do not go crazy over things you cannot control.

I choose pleasure over pain and if I cannot have pleasure then at least I choose NO (minimal) pain.

Good luck on your respective life's journeys.

KABBALISTIC INSIGHTS

In Judaism, the first words we say immediately upon awakening is to recite the short paragraph, "modeh ani l'fanecha." translated as "I am grateful to you, the living Master of the universe who has returned my soul to me with great mercy in your belief in me."

Usually, in order to recite a prayer, we need to wash our hands. The Kabbalistic teachers explain that appreciation and gratitude for God's mercies are so pure and appreciated that hand washing can wait.

TALMUDIC DEBATE vs. PRESIDENTIAL DEBATE

Like everything else in 2020, things do not seem to go right. Case in point: We just witnessed the first presidential debate. I think we can all agree that it was not enjoyable, informative, uplifting or helpful in the slightest. I am not faulting or pointing fingers at any one candidate as this is beyond the pale of this article, and completely beside the point. Debates should not be a slug fest, rather they should be an exchange of ideas and values in an environment of respect, while bearing an open mind to perhaps learn something from someone else.

The debate made me think of other great debates in our history. One debate that comes to mind which was so beautiful to watch was the one between Reagan and Mondale. It was shortly before the 1984 presidential election. Ronald Reagan was asked by the moderator whether his age-he was 73-should be an issue. Reagan answered, "I will not make age an issue of this campaign. I am not going to exploit, for political purposes, my opponent's youth and inexperience." The audience, as well as Reagan's opponent, Walter Mondale, laughed out loud at this response.

Another classy line at another debate was when Lloyd Bentsen in 1988 told freshman Senator Dan Quayle, who remarked that he had as much experience as JFK, "I served with Jack Kennedy. I knew Jack Kennedy. Jack Kennedy was a friend of mine. Senator, you're no Jack Kennedy."

TALMUDIC DEBATES

I then began to reflect on the practice of debates in the Talmud. What transpired was great Jewish scholars and their adherents debated the merits of various laws that had not yet been solidified. They sat across the table from one another and each one gave their reasoning. These debates were conducted with the utmost of respect and love for one another. Take a fascinating look at the most famous of all Talmudic debaters.

SCHOOL OF SHAMMAI vs. SCHOOL OF HILLEL

The House of Hillel and House of Shammai were among Jewish scholars' two schools of thought during the period named after the sages Hillel and Shammai, of the last century BCE and the early 1st century CE, who founded them. These two schools had vigorous debates on matters of ritual practice, ethics, and theology which are the basis of Judaism as it is today.

POLAR OPPOSITES

Both schools differed in their ways of thinking. Most of the time they were at opposite ends. In general, Shammai's positions were stricter than those of Beit Hillel. Take for example the debate on Hannukah lights. Shammai held that on the first night eight lights should be lit, and then they should decrease on each successive night, ending with one on the last night; while Beit Hillel held that one should start with one light and increase the number on each night, ending with eight.

A FASCINATING VICTORY

There is a captivating discussion as to why the final law for the most part ended up to be according to the view of Hillel. It is important to point out that the final law almost always coincided with Hillel, not because his school constituted the majority. In fact, the school of Shammai had a larger number of followers.

The reason given as to why Hillel was handed the victory as the final arbiter of most of the laws (and our presidential debaters should learn a lesson or two from this reason) was because Beit Hillel studied the view of their opponents and did not just dismiss them as wrong, lunacy, dangerous or stupid. Rather, since the school of Hillel was agreeable, humble and patient, it was chosen to lead. More so, the Talmud tells us that not only did the school of Hillel teach Shammai's teachings in addition to their own, they taught them first before their very own opinions!

No, debates do not have to be crude, insensitive, tactless and indelicate. What we learn from these two masters is that a debate should be one of mutual admiration, respect and reverence for the office sought to be held.

KABBALISTIC INSIGHTS

There is a story recorded in the Talmud once Hillel and Shammai disagreed on a legal statute, and fiercely argued over their opinions – each of which they held as deeply true. Just then, a booming voice came forth and proclaimed, "both these and those are the living words of God." (Talmud, Eruvin 13b) Both ideas, though seemingly in conflict, were true at the same time.

208

STOP VACILLATING

THE KABBALAH OF CONVICTION

In politics there is a term that is used quite frequently called "flip flop-ping." It is when a politician says one thing and then changes his/her mind. Remember Bush 41's most famous campaign promise of "no new taxes?" Yet he raised new taxes regardless once elected. Interesting to note though, if a politician apologizes or comes clean about prior policies, then he/she is not a flip flopper, but rather a conscientious politician, as in Michael Bloomberg's case when he apologized for his controversial stop & frisk policy.

This got me thinking. Do we have a parallel concept in Judaism where a flip flopper is redeemed by coming clean?

There is a fascinating lesson to be learned from a strange episode recorded in one of Judaism's most sacred and holy books, Obadia.

ELIJAH THE PROPHET

To make a long story short, the main prophet during the first Temple was Elijah, who singlehandedly undertook the opposition to the wicked King & Queen, Ahab and Jezebel. Elijah came before the king and swore in the name of God that rain would cease to fall in the entire region. This decree would remain in place until he, Elijah, would revoke it. The drought had grown so desperate that Ahab had agreed to meet with Elijah.

THE CHALLENGE

After an initial sharp exchange between the two, Elijah said that if the king wanted any rain to fall, he was to gather all Jewish people on Mount Carmel together with the entire cohort of four hundred and fifty prophets of Baal. The challenge was that both Elijah and the priests of Baal would each offer a sacrifice, but no fire was to be provided. The sacrifice that burned with fire from heaven would prove who the true God really was.

VACILLATORS

The great day of the challenge came and Elijah stepped forward and lambasted the Jewish people with the oddest remark: "How long will you be dancing between two ideas? If the lord is God, go after Him, and if the lord is Baal—go after him!"

STRANGE QUESTION

What a question? Why would he not set the people straight and say pick God? Why even offer them the choice of an idol called Baal? Elijah should have repudiated Baal completely. After all, Baal was a false idol and idol worship is an anathema to the Torah. However, he did not!

POWER ANSWER

Instead, he asked them not to flip flop. He implored them not to vacillate between God and Baal. Choose ONE he said. You see, being a vacillator is much worse than being a person of conviction. Being wishy-washy shows a weak personality and lack of character. Choosing a side is a sign of strength and principle. Winston Churchill stated it best when he proclaimed, "Any decision is better than no decision at all!"

The Kabballah teaches that the problem with a vacillator is that they will never be able to choose the right path. They will always vacillate, hedge their bets and play devil's advocate. Even when shown how wrong they are/were, they will still maintain a certain allegiance to the dark side. Whereas a person with conviction, even with poor judgement, will ultimately be able to see the error of their ways, let go of the bad, apologize and then make things right.

It is imperative for us to learn from Elijah. It is important for us to know right from wrong at all times. Moreover, even though we may be tempted sometimes to do something we are not proud of, we should be at the very least aware that this is not who we really are. This is just a moment of weakness, a mistake, blunder or faux pas.

To err is human. To own up is divine.

KABBALISTIC INSIGHTS

One of the greatest sages to walk this earth often said "Where there are no men, strive to be a man."

One must stand up not only for themselves but also for others and not be wishy washy. The Lubavitcher Rebbe opined something to this effect. If you see something wrong happening in your community, do not say who am I to stand up and make change. Rather than think this way, perhaps this is the reason why you landed in your place of residence and your purpose in this world is to be the one.

NATURE vs. NURTURE

A BEAUTIFUL STORY WITH A POWERFUL LESSON

Last week I received an incredible email from quite a few people. It was a heartwarming story that really tugs on the strings of our emotions. I have not checked the veracity of this story but I am sharing as is since its well worth the read.

THE STORY

"Last week, legendary Laker Kareem Abdul-Jabbar spoke out loudly and forcefully against the pervasive anti-Semitism in Hollywood and professional sports. His condemnation, though refreshing, is not surprising.

You might say goodness runs in the family.

On April 11, 1945, the American Third Army smashed through the gates of the infamous concentration camp known as Buchenwald. The horrors of what they found there shocked soldier and general alike.

Gen. Eisenhower, knowing that one day there would be those who would attempt to deny those horrors ever took place, made the local German population participate in the burial of the thousands of murdered men, women, and children, whose bodies lay exposed throughout the camp.

One of the American liberators was a black man who knew personally the experience of discrimination and hate, and he was profoundly moved.

Seeing a little Jewish boy standing between the survivors, he hoisted him up, and held him high above the heads of the Germans standing there.

'Look at this sweet kid,' he hollered, 'he isn't even eight yet. This was your enemy, he threatened the Third Reich. He is the one against whom you waged war, and murdered millions like him.'

He never forgot what he witnessed. On his deathbed he asked his friend Ferdinand Alcindor to inquire about the boy he had hoisted above his strong shoulders all those years ago. A promise Ferdinand's son would keep in 2011.

Ferdinand's son was born Ferdinand Lewis Alcindor Jr., though you know him as Kareem Abdul-Jabbar. That little Jewish boy who survived Buchenwald would grow up to become the Chief Rabbi of Israel, Rabbi Yisroel Meir Lau." They did meet in 2011.

The person who sent me the story concludes with his own thought, "It truly is about the care you grow up in."

THE LAST LINE

I really enjoyed reading the story he shared, his last line however, made me think and led to this article. He concluded with a statement that it is all about one's upbringing, whether or not you will be a good and sensitive person with morals and values, or a skunk with little to no care about others other than oneself.

THE GREAT DEBATE

Truth be told this is not as simple as it sounds. In fact, it is something that has been debated in many academic circles for over two centuries. Are our personalities predestined or are they the result of our environment? This deliberation is known as the "Nature vs. Nurture" debate, a term coined by Sir Francis Galton in 1871.

NATURE vs. NURTURE BELIEFS

Those on the "nature" side of the debate believe in the idea that an individual's biology is his/her preordained or perpetual destiny, and that it is very difficult to change the innate inborn trait. The "nurture" defenders, on the other hand, reason human behaviors are learned over time. The famous philosopher John Locke argues that the human mind is born as a tabula rasa, or blank slate, with no preconceived innate knowledge.

Where does Judaism stand on this debate?

THE LUBAVITCH REBBE

The Rebbe in a letter completely debunks the "blame the nature argument" and that it is difficult to change an inborn trait. The Rebbe insists that education of values and morals can and will bring the change needed. Essentially, the Rebbe recognizes that we are both nature and nurture. Clearly, he puts great emphasis on the nurture side of things.

In the Rebbe's own pen, "Every day children are born with particular tendencies or drives, some of them good and some of them bad. This is why human beings have to be trained and educated, so as to develop and strengthen the positive characteristics and eliminate the bad ones. The Creator endowed human beings with the capacity to improve, indeed even to change, their 'natural' (i.e., innate) traits."

MAIMONIDES

Maimonides, a Rabbi, author and philosopher who was also acclaimed as the greatest physician of his time, declares in a well-known passage in his famous Code, "Every person has the option (power), if he so desires, to direct himself to do only good and be a Tzaddik, (righteous) or, if he chooses, to follow the bad road and be a Rasha (wicked). Do not ever think that a person is predestined from birth to be a Tzaddik or Rasha. Nor is there any inner compulsion to make a choice, but one has the capacity to choose the right behavior, and it is entirely a matter of one's own will and determination."

Slightly different from the above point of view in that Maimonides completely debunks nature as irrelevant. Who cares if you have a bad trait? Work on it and move on.

TORAH & TALMUD

The Torah records the laws about the wayward and deviant son who does not listen to his father or mother, and is ultimately executed after going through a judicial process.

The Talmud interestingly comments, "There has never been a stubborn and rebellious son convicted and there never will be." If so, why bother to include this law in the Torah?

The answer lies in understanding the complex conditions imposed by the Torah. The boy's mother must be identical to his father in voice, appearance, and height. Both parents' vision must be perfect, they must possess all of their limbs, and the city must have a rabbinical court.

In order for a wayward son to be convicted, the Torah requires that the parents must have identical voices, meaning that he has not received mixed messages. They must be perceived by the child as being totally in control, ruling out parents who are physically or sight handicapped. The city must also be home to a Jewish court that promotes wholesome values.

A child's misbehavior is not a reflection of who he really is. Rather, it reflects his environment. The wrong setting causes him to act out even though he is not naturally inclined to behave badly. So, if the misconduct is due to environment, there is hope for transformation. Change the setting and things are bound to improve.

CONCLUSION

From Judaism's perspective, it is immaterial whether there is nature or nurture. Each and every person have been given gifts and deficiencies. We need to use our gifts for good. We need to make a positive difference. We need to recognize our bad qualities and work on them.

God gave us our free will. Let's use it for good.

KABBALISTIC INSIGHTS

In an excerpt of a letter from the Lubavitcher Rebbe, dated February 4, 1986,

"The fact that the problem may largely be congenital does not alter the situation. Every day children are born with particular natures and innate tendencies or drives, some of them good and some of them bad. This is why human beings have to be trained and educated, so as to develop and strengthen the positive characteristics and eliminate the bad ones.

A case in point is kleptomania. It is generally recognized that kleptomania is a very compulsive drive. But no one will suggest that because it is probably inborn and extremely difficult to resist, the kleptomaniac should be told that it is okay for him to steal, or that there is nothing he can, or should, do about it, and so on"

KABBALAH OF MIRACLES

As a Rabbi, I study many topics of Jewish interest. I have my daily regimen but I also try to study something I have not known (or forgotten) before. In preparing for a lecture series on modern day Israel, I learned quite a few interesting facts that I had not known, and in the process came across a fascinating theme. Namely, miracles.

TWO TYPES OF MIRACLES
UPROOTING NATURE

There are two types of miracles that can occur. The first miracle is one that shatters and defies nature. One example is when God split the sea at the time of Exodus. This miracle took water, which has the tendency to keep on flowing, and caused it to stop flowing and instead started building upon itself into a towering aqua edifice. This caused a literal break in the water and dry land could be seen between the two immense pillars of water.

WITHIN NATURE

The second type of miracle occurs when the natural order is not usurped but rather continues as is. It employs the natural order but is no less miraculous than uprooting nature. The following is an example of a miracle hidden in nature. This took place on Long Island a few years back. This fellow bent down to tie his shoe and at that very moment one of the chains holding the light fixture broke, and the fixture swung back and forth. Because this fellow was on one knee tying his shoelaces, the fixture missed his head by a few inches. The fixture did not disappear as it would have in an open miracle, it swung as any fixture would with a broken chain but caused no harm.

MODERN DAY ISRAEL MIRACLES – YOU BE THE JUDGE

1. UN PARTITION - US

If the U.N. vote which took place on November 29, 1947, had been postponed a mere few months, chances are the modern Israel where Jews can find refuge from all corners of the world would not have happened.

After President Rooscvclt passed and was succeeded by Harry Truman, no one knew that this man was going to be such an incredible friend to the Jews and Israel. President Truman, despite pressure from his own State Department and Pentagon, lobbied for the U.N. partition. And when the new state was declared in May 1948, he extended diplomatic relations immediately.

Just a short few months later when the Cold War got underway, President Truman would not have the flexibility to disregard his own Pentagon advisors who were clearly no fans of the Jewish state.

2. UN PARTITION – USSR

One of strangest twists of irony is that while Great Britain, India, Greece and Cuba voted against the partition, one of the strongest voices of support came from Josef Stalin of the Soviet Union. While he was a staunch anti-Semite, he saw Zionism as a way of pushing Great Britain out of the area. One of the greatest speeches of support at the U.N was by soviet deputy foreign minister Andrei Gromyko.

Just a short few weeks later (January 1948) Stalin had Jewish actor Solomon (Shloyme) Mikhoels assassinated and began his anti-Semitic reign of terror against Jews. Stalin himself came up with the Doctors Plot which essentially claimed that doctors, who were mostly Jewish, were killing soviet leaders.

It really was a unique moment in time.

3. ALTALENA

Although the ship called Altalena met with an unhappy ending, and if not for Menachem Begin would probably have led to a Jewish civil war, the story of Altalena's origin is nothing short of miraculous. For reasons that we can only speculate, the country of France, with approval of the French Foreign Minister Georges Bidault, donated 153 million francs worth of weapons to the Jewish members of the Irgun to be brought to Israel.

It is unclear how much weaponry was salvaged after David Ben Gurion ordered it to be destroyed. We do know however, that the Altalena carried close to 950 Freedom Fighters to Israel. According to historians at least two million rounds of ammunition, 3,000 shells, and 200 Bren guns were brought into Israel.

France had been supportive of Israel until 1967 when it came as a shock when Charles de Gaulle uttered these famous words, "France had freed itself … from the very special and very close ties with Israel," complaining that Jews were "an elite people, sure of itself, and dominating." It was very clear to all that France had formed an alliance with many Arab countries and joined the arms embargo against Israel. It was nothing short of a miracle that back then France was instrumental in getting Israel off the ground.

These are just some of the "miracles" clothed within nature that occurred in the early days when Israel needed it most. I am a total believer that these events are just as awe inspiring as...... the splitting of the sea, rising of the sun, the gravitational pull of the moon, Saddam Hussein's 30 scud rockets to Israel that fell harmlessly or the creation of the world.

I anticipate miracles. Do you?

KABBALISTIC INSIGHTS

There is a great debate as to whether miracles that manipulate nature are greater or not. The Kabbalistic insight on this is that a miracle that obliviates nature while an incredible feat, is nothing compared to a miracle that is clothed in nature, where it uses nature itself to accomplish its miracles. It is so hidden that many people do not even realize what happened.

CORONA COGITATIONS

UNSEEN AND UNKNOWN

A COVID THOUGHT

I was in the airport recently dropping someone off. It was the first time in many months that I had been in an airport building and what I saw both astounded and saddened me.

I saw an empty — and I mean empty — terminal with literally no one around other than a few passengers and a lot more Port Authority employees. I witnessed closed stores and shops, and those that were open had no customers. It was depressing to see and a part of me was frightened and agitated. I mean if this airport is a microcosm of what is going on, then how will we ever recover from this unknown and unseen virus.

As a student of Chassidic philosophy, I was taught that everything that we encounter and anything that crosses our path should be viewed as a life lesson. So, I asked myself what on earth can I glean from living through this pandemic.

I have written about some of the positive effects of COVID-19, such as appreciating having a home, resetting priorities and acknowledging heroes, such as first responders in our midst. The problem though is that as COVID-19 rages on, these silver lining type clichés can get stale and become underwhelming.

After exiting the airport feeling down, an epiphany struck me and I quickly jotted this fleeting thought whilst standing at the street crossing.

This humongous transportation hub that houses one of the busiest airports in the country has been reduced to a shadow of its former self. It has gone from being alive, prosperous, insanely busy, incredibly important and vital to a limited crew and a small airport feel. What caused this horrific downfall? Something that is invisible to the naked eye and an unknown entity. Wild stuff. An invisible energy that can only be measured in a scientific lab brings down Gotham!

Viewing this from a Chassidic lens, I said to myself, "If something microscopic can cause such destruction, then this must also be true in the affirmative, and other microscopic things can rebuild." You see, things do not only work one way. If they exist in the negative, then they must also exist in the positive and vice versa. Take fire as an example. Fire can destroy a life but fire can also save a life. An army can kill but it also protects.

There are some positive energies in the world that are mighty, yet most people dismiss them as being insignificant, and they are often overlooked. Some seem to be trivial and are invisible in terms of importance.

Here are examples of magnanimous and life-altering things you can do that are so small, yet incredibly powerful, and wholly capable of creating positive energy.

A good morning to a homeless person can make this human being feel normal and be so uplifting and hopeful that he or she yearns to live another day.

Assisting an elderly person pack her car after a run to the grocery store and offering to return the cart so that she does not have to.

Saying thank you to the person who filled your car with fuel, the grocery bagger or the mail carrier.

We are taught that it is the everyday, seemingly inconsequential things that catch God's eye. The reason being when an everyday minor act of kindness is performed; it is specifically this that arouses His mercies. We send a small signal up to God and He responds in greater measure.

And by God, we need all the mercy, compassion and love we can get.

Be safe and kind.

KABBALISTIC INSIGHTS

The great Kabbalist, The Tzemach Tzedek had an axiom "Think good and it will be good."

He explains as follows "A person must speak and act in a positive manner, and a matching attitude will become permanently lodged in his heart.

Accordingly, God will arouse a merciful spirit upon him with joy and gladness of heart ..."

LESSONS OF COVID-19
THE GOOD, THE BAD AND THE UGLY

Many years ago, I happened perchance to meet Clint Eastwood in Carmel, California, and I asked him what was his favorite Clint Eastwood movie at the time. I am not such a movie buff so I figure when my Yeshiva lets out, I will watch one or two that have highly recommended. He responded that he really enjoyed *The Good, the Bad and the Ugly*.

The movie struck this 20-year-old as sometimes the good can also be bad and vice versa. This got me to reflect on our current situation where things seem to be going from bad to ugly. Perhaps there is good as well if we look at it differently.

BAD

There is clearly a lot going on in this country.

We have a pandemic that wreaked havoc. There are over two million recorded cases and it has killed close to 113,000 Americans. There are still so many sick and from those who have recovered, there are many who are very sick with other ailments which were caused by COVID-19. Because of COVID-19 we have high unemployment numbers, though it varies from state to state. The average is 13% compared to historic lows just last year. We also have businesses closed and some will not reopen as they could not weather the storm. In addition, we have kids at home because schools are closed, which of course adds fuel to the fire of many parents not being able to work and kids going insane from being cooped up for so long.

All houses of worship are closed (slowly reopening), which means that our spiritual support is lacking and the community feeling is nonexistent. It is not a pretty sight that is for sure.

GOOD

We have witnessed so much good. We must not only focus on the bad. In my opinion, I can count at least a half dozen good things that have grown out of this horrific pandemic.

SELF SACRIFICE: Just think of every health care worker, from doctors to nurses to phlebotomists to hospital janitors. What remarkable people they are. They literally go into the lion's den every day while everyone else is quarantined. They have to be on their game constantly for sometimes 18 hours straight. They have to wear PPE equipment all day and some of them have chosen to social distance from their own families. Extraordinary people really.

CARING PEOPLE: I always knew most people are good. I experienced this personally when I had seniors who were either afraid or could not go to the supermarket to pick up necessities. I put out a call saying I need help, and I got inundated by so many people who were eager to shop for a stranger. How beautiful.

SCHOLARSHIP: As a Rabbi I offer classes on Judaism a couple of times a week and there are a handful of people who take me up on it and schlep out to The Chai Center to gain more knowledge of their heritage. Because of COVID-19, I have been giving classes on Facebook and Zoom. There are some classes that get thousands of views which tells me that there is a thirst for knowledge and scholarship. Think about it. Thousands of people who normally do not shlep to a class are now studying. For an online schedule, go to TheChaiCenter.com.

INTROSPECTION: With many of us stuck at home, we have temporarily lost the identities we had in the outside world. The pandemic has given us space and time to connect with who we really are. This is similar to the concept of the Jewish day of rest, Shabbat. It is a day where we focus on ourselves and those we care about. During this pandemic, we have the opportunity to reflect on ourselves more than we had done in the past.

PRIORITIES: I am not talking toilet paper. I am still scratching my head on that one. Regardless of one's own sense of essentials, it is clear that what we really thought was important that we could not live without, has now been reframed and priorities have shifted. An immediate example that comes to mind: I think of some of my friends whose entire life is sports. We have learned that we can live without sports for a while. Netflix has taken its place. Oy vey.

LIFE: I left this for last. We have been made keenly aware that life is fragile. We need to cherish life, family, friends, community and not take anyone or anything for granted. We even closed the doors of synagogues because it is so precious. While you may not be able to see your parent, family or friends, you can still call and check up on them. Most importantly, live life and love life. Do not let the doldrums get you down. Breathe the air and thank God you are alive.

UGLY

I would be remiss if we did not bring up the ugly.

This country is divided and it is not good. I see the comments on Facebook, the cursing out of one another over things that the combaters can do nothing about other than verbally abuse each other. I have experienced it myself. I write something and people jump down my throat because I worded it this way and not the way they would have worded the article. It is terrible. I no longer listen to talk radio or any of the slanted news channels. I do so in protest as they are causing (intentionally worded) the hatred of one human to another. To those who hate without help, then they are exacerbating the division that already exists.

If we have learned one thing from this virus and pandemic it would be the following. This Coronavirus is blind to cultural and ideological differences, infecting people of all races, religions, and ages. It does not matter to this invisible bug who you are voting for in the next election!

We need to coalesce and be open to disagreeing without the vitriol. We can have differing of opinions without being called names and ridiculed.

We need to learn to agree to disagree without being disagreeable.

KABBALISTIC INSIGHTS

The deeper teachings of Torah convey that the way we see affects the things we are viewing! (sounds similar to Quantum Theory).

One example, someone with pure thoughts and intention creates a positive energy when looking or interacting with something. It is true with opposite as well. Negativity breeds negativity.

WHAT DOES POST QUARANTINE LOOK LIKE?

LESSONS FOR A "NEW LIFE"

While Long Island has not technically opened up yet, it is very apparent to all that the local roads are getting busier and the Long Island Expressway even more so. Now that New Jersey and Connecticut have begun easing restrictions as well as other parts of New York State, it is becoming more flexible in what the general public is allowed to do.

This past Sunday, I was driving on the freeway and I actually had to slow down because of the number of vehicles on the road, which was a surprise because it has been free flowing lately. This act of putting my foot on the brake pedal for a moment led to the following thoughts.

WHAT HAPPENED

Life as we knew it stopped. The hustle and bustle of dropping off and picking up the kids came to a screeching halt. The mad dash to the bus, train and ferry turned into an extra hour of sleep. The dream of working from your home in pajamas became a reality. The concern of being fired may actually happen now, or worse, happened. You went from a sharp dresser to a t-shirt and shorts type of guy. You stopped shopping from Amazon for clothes but are now using it to find hand soap and sanitizer as well as Lysol wipes. Basically, our lives became surreal, topsy-turvy and insane.

NOT SO FAST

Hold on. Was life not insane before? The running to get this done, that done and the other done all by 11 AM is also by definition insanity. The sleepless nights, the work-related agate, the relentless homework frustrations, the abusive boss and the jealous co-workers were not healthy to begin with. I would be so bold to say that if one was unable to go to their child's elementary school because the boss insisted that your presence at the staff meeting was a must, then maybe this job isn't worth it and the fact that you got fired is a true blessing. I could go on and on. Don't get me wrong, I have full empathy for those who lost their job, even temporarily. I am just throwing out food for thought.

BACK TO NORMAL

My further thinking (which completely distracted my driving) led me to ask myself the following natural follow through question. Do we want to go back to normal? Does normal even make sense? Furthermore, was normal even normal or was it abnormal? (See why I got distracted).

WHAT WILL HAPPEN

I am not a prophet and I have no idea what the future will hold. I will offer this though. If we simply go back to the rat race where we are stressed ad nauseum and the pursuit of the holy dollar dictates our lives, then we have missed an opportunity. I despise COVID-19–19. I hate quarantine. I cry for those lost, especially for the 40 or so people that I knew personally. However, I do recognize that as hard as it has been, and once again, I do not know what the future holds, I have learned that the previous pre-corona life was by and large full of self-imposed flaws and a disservice to me, my family and to all of us.

GOING FORWARD – THE PRACTICAL

We need to reassess our values. Who says we need to own suits from Nordstrom or outfits from Neiman Marcus? Maybe work from home a couple days a week instead of catching the 5:54 AM Metro North to NYC. Go catch a 7 AM morning minyan those days and then go to the home office. You get the idea. If Covid-19 taught us anything in 2020 it is that what was once so vastly important and integral to your very life, you managed mainly without it for the past few months.

Whether or not you believe that we only live once - definitely make this life count.

KABBALISTIC INSIGHTS

Cheshbon HaNefesh, literally translated as "accounting of the soul." Is essentially dedicating time of deep contemplation and reflection of our recent past.

There was this great sage Rabbi Menachem Mendel Lefin of Satanov (1749–1826), who kept a journal to document so he can reflect if he wronged anyone.

THE RETURN TO NORMALCY

THOUGHTS ON RACISM

Both Governors of New York and New Jersey have begun to start loosening up restrictions and both states have entered what they call Phase II.

After a lockdown of close to 100 days, many businesses are now open, including restaurants and shops, albeit with restrictions. Houses of worship are now allowed up to 25% of their capacity. It seems that we have turned a corner, but the future is somewhat on shaky ground as we are not sure what lies ahead. Some parts of New York will enter Phase III in a couple of days which will further relax restrictions to allow indoor dining and that elusive massage.

In an article from a few weeks ago, I decried that the normal life we had pre-COVID-19 was anything but normal. Our lives were insane, way too busy, with not enough downtime and family time and nowhere near enough spiritual nurturing. I posed the following questions. Will we ever get back to normal? Do we even want to get back to normal? Was normal normal or was normal abnormal?

After this lockdown where we have had time to reflect and hopefully do plenty of introspection, we need to rethink as a nation the harsh issue of racism. As a Rabbi, I am obligated to teach Torah and truths. The following would be the Torah's teachings.

IMAGE OF GOD

Every human being of every race, color, creed, faith and ethnicity is created in God's image. Each one of us is created for a specific purpose. Not one person was created as redundant. There is no such thing as alternates or understudies as in a jury or theater. We all have something to offer and no one is allowed to put down another unless it is in a court of law. To be clear, any racism and inequality that we have witnessed does not have a holy platform to stand on and is rejected wholeheartedly by Judaism.

Yes, racism does exist. The black community has been especially hit hard. They feel excluded, picked on and treated harsher than other ethnic groups and this is a tragedy and needs to stop. The executions of George Floyd and Rashard Brooks should never have happened. The protests that we have witnessed or been a part of are very telling. People, of all diversities, want racism to end. Completely. The looting, violence that we have seen is not to be confused with the peaceful protesters.

LAW AND ORDER

One of the seven Torah laws given to all nations is the law of officers and judges and a fair impartial court system. It is a fundamental required to assure that there is law and order and not chaos and anarchy (think Noah's flood). What most people are protesting is in fact that they want law and order. We do not want police officers to act as an officer, judge, jury, bailiff and warden. We want a proper and appropriate system to ensure that people who are created in the image of God be treated fairly.

POLICE TEAM

I feel strongly that social workers, therapists, addiction specialists and psychologists be part of the active police force who come out to the scene when a call comes in. In San Diego, the police force has officers who have been trained in mental illness and it is a special unit that responds to a call that involves potential suicides, violent children, abuse, etc. I cannot imagine a police force without it. Let's not defund the police as this goes against Torah, but rather let's expand the police with a myriad of professionals who are experts in respect and are able to navigate turbulent waters.

PAST HISTORY

We must learn from history. It is no secret that Jewish communities globally do not always get along with one another. There are various disagreements and philosophical differences which sometimes (hopefully rare) can lead to blatant hostilities. Whenever I hear of two Jewish people fight or argue against one another due to some philosophical difference, I think to myself, the Nazis could care less what your stand is on one thing or another. They did not care what type of Jew you were and where you stood on the totem pole of Jewish life. They did not distinguish between secular, liberal, conservative, atheist or traditional. They simply killed you because you were a Jew.

We need to learn from this. We are all human beings. We must not create rifts and hatred because of the color of someone's skin or their origin of birth. We must learn from the Nazis' hate to completely distance ourselves from racism, bigotry and discrimination. Nazism failed as it should. Racism will fail as it should.

PRESENT HISTORY

The Coronavirus did not discriminate either. It got ALL people sick. It killed human beings from all backgrounds, all races, all creeds, every ethnicity and philosophy. It was/is a global pandemic. No one was immune. It did not care what your gender was. It did not care if you were liberal or conservative. Let's learn from past and present history. We need to show no disparity between each other just like this virus did.

RETURN TO NORMALCY

I do not want things to go back to normal. I want things to be much better than they were. I am hoping that by the time we do reach Phase III, the riots and violence have stopped and that there is a global hug filled with warmth, understanding and respect for all. We need for this to happen in order to move on to a post-COVID-19 future where we rebuild the world after the decimation that we all lived through.

Wishful thinking? Up to us.

KABBALISTIC INSIGHTS

"Recognizing the unnatural environment of prison and the bizarre, tragic realities faced by the families of prisoners, the Lubavitcher Rebbe urged the introduction of Torah study, prayer, and Torah-commandment performance to the prisoners and their families.

Responding to this mandate, the Aleph Institute organized trained rabbis and volunteers utilizing audio-visual equipment, books, and Torah-commandment paraphernalia (such as phylacteries and prayer shawls) to bring the Torah way of life into prisons.

More than ten thousand men and women and their families have been exposed to Torah study, Torah-commandment observance, and prayer with various levels of intensity." Rabbi Shalom D. Lipskar - Aleph

JEWISH VIEW ON VACCINATION

During the last month of 2020 companies have had the vaccine against Covid 19 approved. The first was Pfizer, then Moderna and finally AstraZeneca. More will be forthcoming in the very near future.

OBJECTIONS ON RELIGIOUS GROUNDS

I know that there are many people who object to any vaccine on religious grounds. This is more prominent in Scientology, etc. In Judaism however, there are many reasons as to why one should take the vaccine. I will discuss them shortly.

In 2019, there was an uproar in the ultra-Orthodox Brooklyn and Rockland communities. Many of these parents refused to vaccinate their kids against measles. The reason they cited was "religious fatalism," a term I had never heard before. After looking up the meaning, I learned that it was the belief that God is in control of the illness rather than a vaccine.

THE SAGES TAKE

Most Sages agree that guarding one's health is not only a good idea, it is a Mitzvah. This means that whether you like it or not, it is a command, and therefore, you must abide. Greats like Maimonides and the first Chabad Rebbe both emphasize that our body is a gift from

God, and therefore we need to protect it at all costs. At all costs means that even if the virus one is exposed to did not harm 99 people, the 100th person still needs to protect themselves from exposure and take preventative measures such as leaving the city where the virus is located, or taking a vaccine in case there is nowhere to run, like in a pandemic.

Another great thinker, Rabbi Yisroel Lipschutz, who passed in 1860, ruled that despite the risk of death from the smallpox vaccine, one should still be vaccinated. These days the death rate from the smallpox vaccine is so miniscule that it is much safer than Tylenol.

The Lubavitcher Rebbe in 1957 urged people to take the polio vaccine.

KOSHER

There are concerns about non-kosher ingredients, and therefore objections. This too has been dealt with considerably in Jewish law. It has been determined that it is totally acceptable to inject a non-kosher vaccine as a preventative or inject medication as a cure. Even a pig's valve to replace one's own mitral valve or aortic valve is considered kosher.

POSSIBILITY OF DANGER

In Judaism, we learn that if there is a dash of concern that by doing a certain mitzvah, one could get harmed, then one is exempt. Take for example, someone who is sick and the doctors tell him that it is deleterious to your health if you fast even on Yom Kippur, then the individual is forbidden to fast. In fact, if he does fast then he is considered a sinner! Of course, this law can be turned around and one can make the argument that a vaccine without 10 years of research is unsafe.

ISRAEL

I find it interesting that in Israel the COVID vaccine is being given at faster rates than any other country in the world. I am told that they even give the vaccine on Shabbat because of overriding danger. New York could learn a thing or two from Israel. In my opinion, we should be dispensing this vaccine 24/7. Let us not waste a minute.

RESPONSIBILITY

I firmly believe that it is the responsibility of each person to take all and any measures to stop COVID. It is our duty, a mitzvah, obligation, burden and privilege to be an active participant in its eradication. As the great Rabbi Hillel said, "If I am only for myself, then who am I."

We do not live in a bubble. Isolation and quarantining for another 100 days has been proven that it is not the answer and neither is it practical.

I meet many people in the course of a week, and I know that at any moment I can get or spread this diabolical virus. I probably will have to wait a while to receive the vaccine myself. However, when the day comes, I will arrive early for my appointment.

We need to beat this and we will, with God's help and with yours.

If you decide not to take the vaccine, I will not respect you less or feel negative toward you. I don't think someone can be forced to do something against his or her will. I disagree with you for the above-mentioned reasons, but I won't be disagreeable.

KABBALISTIC INSIGHTS

A traditional vaccine entails injecting a strain of a virus into the body, in order for the body to fight it and develop immunity. Similar is the idea of someone that erred and then repented. Seeing, hearing or doing something negative and then completely rejecting it can inoculate one against further transgressions.

GLOSSARY OF TERMS

ARIZAL: Rabbi Isaac Luria Ashkenazi, was a leading rabbi and Jewish mystic in the community of Safed in the Galilee region of Israel.

CHABAD: Chabad is one of the world's best-known Hasidic movements, particularly for its outreach activities, headquartered in Crown Heights, Brooklyn. There are over 5,000 outposts over the globe.

CHANUKAH: The Jewish festival of lights commemorating the miracle of the oil and the miraculous defeat of the Greek army, which then allowed the restoration of the Holy Temple in Jerusalem.

CHASSIDIC: A mystical Jewish movement founded the 1800's. There are many sects, and each sect has a leader or Rebbe. The largest and most well-known are the Lubavitch Chassidim.

LUBAVITCH: Synonymous with Chabad.

MISHNA: Is the first major body of work on Jewish Law. It is the first book called the Oral Torah.

MITZVAH: A Biblical or Rabbinical Commandment. Also loosely translated as any good deed.

PURIM: Rabbinical Jewish holiday commemorating the victory in Persia over the wicked Haman and his cohorts.

SABBATH: The Jewish day of Rest.

SATMAR: A Hasidic group originating from a city in Hungary. Now headquartered in Williamsburg, Brooklyn.

SHAVUOT: Biblical Jewish Holiday commemorating the giving of the Torah on Mt. Sinai.

TALMUD: A clarification and elucidation of the Mishna in long form.

TANYA: An early work of the first Lubavitch Rebbe, Rabbi Shneur Zalman.

TORAH: Usually referred to as the five books of Moses, however many use it to include a much broader view, i.e., Books of Prophets, Writings. Others use this term in a very general sense, referring to anything Jewish written, as long the author is God fearing.

TEFILLIN: Also called Phylacteries. It is a set of small black leather boxes containing scrolls of parchment inscribed with verses from the Torah. Tefillin are worn every weekday by men and boys over the age of 13 usually during morning prayers.

TZIZIT: Tzitzit are specially knotted ritual fringes, attached to the four corners of a wearable garment called a Tallit.

YESHIVA: Jewish day school.